THE FRENCH KITCHEN COOKBOOK

THE FRENCH KITCHEN COOKBOOK

RECIPES AND LESSONS FROM PARIS AND PROVENCE

PATRICIA WELLS

Photographs by Jeff Kauck

WILLIAM MORROW
An Imprint of HarperCollinsPublishers

FIRST EDITION

Design by Lorie Pagnozzi

Library of Congress Cataloging-in-Publication Data has been applied for.

ISBN 978-0-06-208891-8

13 14 15 16 17   ID6/RRD   10 9 8 7 6 5 4 3 2 1

As many times before, this book is for Walter.
For his incredible patience, his appetite for all the good
things in life, his support, companionship, fidelity,
friendship. The best husband a woman could have!

When restoring my Paris studio in 1995, I found these 1890s oak and beveled glass doors from a Paris café, with much of the lettering still intact.

CONTENTS

INTRODUCTION

My cooking school, At Home with Patricia Wells, came about like this: As we sat around the dinner table with family and friends in Paris and Provence, guests would constantly quiz me. "Tell me about sea salt," one guest would begin. Another would beg me to explain the cycle of the olive and the process of making of olive oil. Some wanted to know why a Châteauneuf-du-Pape wine rated higher than a Gigondas. And then there were market questions: How do you know when an eggplant, a tomato, a zucchini, is at its peak of ripeness?

I would then give a brief but hopefully informative response, but I soon began to think about expanding what was already a pretty full career in food. As restaurant critic for the *International Herald Tribune* and author of several guidebooks and many cookbooks, I already had plenty on my plate. But our haven in Provence—the eighteenth-century farmhouse known as Chanteduc—begged to be shared. It also begged to hear even more sounds of laughter, friendship, and good times in the kitchen and garden and around the table.

So in 1995 we were ready to test the idea of a cooking school, one much like the memorable weeklong classes I had attended years before with Marcella Hazan and other illustrious teachers. But I did wonder: Would anyone come? Would we even enjoy doing it? We began with just two weeklong classes that September, and since then we have never looked back.

If I made a list of our hundred closest friends, a good number of them would have started out as students—strangers before they found their way up the hill to our ancient Provençal *mas*, or into the courtyard and up the stairs to my cooking stu-

1

dio in Paris. Soon we began to realize that we must be doing something right, for students came back again and again, as many as six or seven times. Over the years, we expanded and contracted, adding Paris classes in my cooking studio on Rue Jacob in the 6th arrondissement, conducting special weeks to study truffles, wine, fish, and shellfish, and to balance food and fitness. We even took the school "off campus" several times, conducting weeklong classes in Florence, Venice, Verona, and Vietnam.

This book is a compilation and reflection on what we've learned, the students and I, as we have prepared meals together. What joys people experience as they accomplish something they never imagined they would: the overwhelming feeling of satisfaction from the preparation of a perfect fruit tart; the pleasure of extracting a warm, fragrant, golden brioche from the oven; the giddiness of sharing a meal with a group of former strangers who quickly become lifelong friends.

This is a cookbook, of course, but it is just as much about my life in cooking, the way I instruct, the way I organize, the way I anticipate, the way I direct, the way I collect, the way I constantly test and retest and experiment. It is about simplicity, it is about complexity. But all in all, it is about a way of life and a lifestyle of food and entertaining.

There are days when we want a challenge in cooking as well as the exhilaration of making a truly memorable wintry beef *daube*, a stunning tomato *tatin* that captures wows from the guests at the table, gorgeous puff pastry cheese wands that could grace the window of Paris's finest pastry shop. We are willing to devote the time and effort in exchange for the anticipated reward.

Then there are days when we just want to get dinner on the table in a matter of minutes, turning to a quick sirloin carpaccio or a salmon sashimi, an instant thin-crust pizza that can be made in less than thirty minutes start to finish, a sorbet that takes seconds to make and comes to a rich and delicate life of its own as we sit down at the table.

In my classes, I like to offer students both choices, as I offer them myself daily. Many days, nothing gives me greater pleasure than to rise early, go through my routine of hiking, running, treadmill, or whatever it is that day, then spend the day in the kitchen. Testing, retesting, creating, inventing. And then there are days when I don't have a second to think about cooking: Maybe it's a day of errands, appointments, and so on, and when dinnertime comes, I really haven't a clue. That's when I turn to the instant-pleasure recipes that are included here.

Over the years, I have watched as total novices in the kitchen are transformed into confident cooks, and beam as they and their fellow students put together a veritable seasonal feast. Almost all my students are eager amateurs willing to learn any *truc* that will lead to greater success and satisfaction in the kitchen.

I don't lecture, but I do make it clear that certain rules should be followed in the kitchen. Here are a few of the most important:

LEARNING TO COOK: Over the years, novices have asked me quite simply, "But how do I learn to cook?" I tell them to sit down and make a list of the ten things they most love to eat. It may be French fries or a lemon tart. A perfect puff pastry or chocolate cake. I suggest the list be varied (not all desserts, please). Then, as though you are a pianist learning to play a piece of music, you cook, cook, cook! Practice that first recipe until you feel you have mastered it, or at least have made it taste as good as you think you can at this point. Then move on to the second recipe on the list, and so on. By the time you have reached the tenth recipe, you will have a basic repertoire. Then, of course, make another list of ten and continue the process.

READ THE RECIPE: Most mistakes are made by not reading the recipe carefully or visualizing the final product. I take great care in recipe writing (and constant rewriting) to make every step as clear as possible, making it easier on everyone, giving us all a chance of success in the end.

MISE EN PLACE: meaning "everything in place." In my cooking school as well as when I am cooking by myself, recipes are enclosed in a small plastic folder, and all ingredients are measured and set out neatly on a tray. This way, if I use up the last egg or drop of vanilla extract, those ingredients are instantly written out on the shopping list hanging in the kitchen. *Mise en place* means the cook has not only weighed, measured, washed, and chopped, but has checked the recipe for any missing ingredients, lined up equipment such as spatulas and blenders, and preheated the oven if necessary. *Mise en place* also makes for a neater kitchen, and I find that when the kitchen is neat, there is less chance for disaster or hysteria. (There's another advantage to all that premeasuring and collecting of ingredients: If you put something in the oven and turn around to find you've forgotten an important ingredient, you can most likely go back to the drawing board and repair any potential mistakes.)

USE THE RIGHT KNIFE OR PAN FOR THE TASK: Over and over again I find that students choose a knife too small for the task, or a pan that is much too skimpy for whatever is to be cooked in it. I don't know if it is out of a sense of economy, but I always suggest cooks visualize what the end product should look like and go from there.

TASTE, TASTE, TASTE: Often a student will come to me, proudly presenting his or her creation, and when I ask, "Did you taste it?," more often than not, the answer is no.

COLD FOR COLD, HOT FOR HOT: My freezer always holds small teacups used for serving sorbets, and before preparing cold soups I also place shallow soup bowls in the freezer so at serving time there is no loss of that precious chilled temperature. A warming drawer is always at hand so that hot food can be served on hot plates, but an oven on low heat (250°F; 130°C) will suffice.

MENU PLANNING: I put a lot of emphasis on seasonal menu planning. In fact, with each week's class I try to work each and every totally seasonal ingredient into the mix, including fish and shellfish, fruits and vegetables, meats and herbs. In the summer, I almost always start with a cold soup, most of which can be prepared ahead of time. A vegetarian menu might be centered around my favorite "pizza pasta," penne that's teamed up with my favorite pizza topping of tomatoes, olives, artichokes, and capers.

From the beginning, my goal is for the students to leave the class eager and ready to make every dish we create during the week. There is nothing worse than tasting something and saying to yourself, "This is okay, but I wouldn't make it again." So there are many crowd-pleasers, but both simple and complex, ranging from a quick but very doable puff pastry to easy-as-pie dessert squares made with fragrant chestnut honey and almonds.

BEST TASTE OF THE WEEK AND TAKEAWAYS: At the end of our final meal on Friday, everyone gets to vote on Best Taste of the Week. At the same time, I ask students about their takeaway from the week, the one *truc* or idea, concept or cooking skill, that will remain with them long after we've parted ways.

Interestingly, tops on the Best Taste of the Week list are always soups (both cold and warm) and sorbets. Many perennial favorite recipes are included here (such as the Miniature Onion and Goat Cheese *Tatins*; the Tomato Trio of Yellow Tomato Soup with Evergreen Tomato *Tartare* and Red Tomato Sorbet; Tomato *Tatins*; Eggplant in Spicy Tomato Sauce with Feta; Mussels with Lemon, Capers, Jalapeño, and Cilantro; Open Ravioli with Mushrooms; Saffron and Honey Brioche; and Chestnut Honey Squares).

In all classes we focus on the simple (but often mishandled) craft of the proper cutting of vegetables, and for many students that's a big takeaway of the week. Another technique I try to instill in students' minds is what I call the "cold pan technique." Rather than placing oil or butter in a pan, heating it up, and then adding, say, minced garlic or chopped onions, I add the oil, garlic, onions, and a touch of salt all together and "sweat" the entire combination, covered, over low heat to form a soft and succulent flavor base for the rest of the recipe to come. This priceless tip is always at the top of the takeaway list, along with the ease of making a multiple variety of sorbets; the use of a steamer, and steaming on a bed of herbs; the joys of cooking with a good copper pan; and of course the all-important *mise en place*. Best of all, students leave with a newfound sense of confidence in the kitchen.

WINE: Wine plays a big role in our lives and in the cooking school as well. When students arrive for the first day's class, a crisp new white apron embroidered with their name awaits them, along with a booklet of recipes with the program for the week. I tell them that the most important page in the book is the Importers List on the very last page (here on page 299). Over the years I have found that there are a dozen or so United States importers—among them our own Clos Chanteduc importer, Eric Solomon, and longtime friend Kermit Lynch—whom I respect and whose taste in wine I share. I tell everyone, if you want to learn about wine, go to your local wine store (or stores) with the list and simply ask: "What wines do you have from any of these importers?" Take half a dozen bottles home, and taste these wines. You'll be sure to find something you like. Repeat this enough times, and soon you'll have a more educated, well-rounded wine palate. Not to mention the pleasures of the exercise! And please don't forget the all-important "proper" wineglass. It does not have to be fancy or expensive, just large enough to swirl, add a bit of air to the wine, and open it up for fuller tasting and pleasure.

AESTHETICS: For cooking to be truly pleasurable for me, it must be aesthetic. I pay careful attention to each knife, bowl, pan, and utensil in my kitchen. Some objects are loved for nostalgic reasons (a wonderful worn chopping board made by my father-in-law a half-century ago), others for their sheer efficiency (a serrated tomato knife, a thin and sleek ceramic knife for chopping, an all-purpose knife we bought for about a dollar in Vietnam, yet worth its weight in gold).

I like work bowls to be white and ceramic and if at all possible made by a potter I know. The connection between the maker and the user can be strong and powerful and can add even more pleasure to the cooking process itself.

At the table, I follow suit. I rarely use patterned linens or tableware, for I prefer solid colors—preferably crisp white—to serve as a clean, uncluttered, noncompetitive background for the food.

COLLECTIONS: I am a collector: white porcelain pots for cooking, a battery of colorful *mise en place* bowls for the kitchen, cutting boards and well-worn containers for butcher's string, even a set of metal pastry scrapers found in a flea market in Florence. It's not just that all these objects are practical and useful; they add a touch of pleasure to the day-to-day cooking process. Over the years I have gathered an extensive collection of table linens, napkin rings, knife rests, embroidered napkins, and place mats. I do sometimes go a bit overboard with detail (rabbit knife rests for a rabbit dish; napkins colorfully embroidered with various poultry to use when serving chicken, duck, squab, or guinea fowl), but as the saying goes, "God is in the details," and the more one pays attention to what's on the plate and on the table, the more everyone gets from the overall experience.

PARIS OR PROVENCE?: The school year begins in January in Provence, with my favorite class of all, the Black Truffle Extravaganza. In spring, we generally offer three weeklong classes in Paris, then several early and late summer classes in Provence.

The recipes in this book reflect what we cook in both Paris and Provence. Most of the appetizers can be made in any season, so appear on the menus in both places. The long spring asparagus season means we can use the first-of-season vegetables from late February to June to prepare the favored Provençal Lemon-Braised Asparagus. Spring in Paris will always mean Yveline's Chilled Cucumber and Avocado Soup with Avocado Sorbet, as well as the refreshing Salmon Sashimi with an Avalanche of Herbs. From summer through autumn all the tomato favorites appear on the table in Provence, along with the recipes that include mussels, eggplant, fennel, and zucchini.

In the end, no matter where we are cooking together, it really is all about the joys of combining good food, good wine, and friends all together around the table. The sensory experience is available to all of us, and my motivation as a journalist and a teacher is to enhance that experience—one we can enjoy day in and day out, anytime.

A WORD ABOUT THE PHOTOS IN THIS BOOK: This is the Wells/Kauck team's third project together, and for this book we photographed at both our home in Provence and my cooking studio in Paris. As ever, we tried to make the food look as simple and appealing as possible. Everything is photographed in natural light with plates, utensils, tableware, and linens from my own collections.

The crew: photographer Jeff Kauck, Patricia Wells, editorial assistant Emily Buchanan, photo assistant Dana Kauck, editor Walter Wells, food stylist Sue Kauck.

OPENING ACTS

HAM AND CHEESE SQUARES
WITH CORNICHONS 11

ONION AND GRUYÈRE BITES 13

SAUTÉED DATES WITH FENNEL
AND WALNUTS 15

ANCHOVY BITES 16

ANCHOVY CREAM 19

CURRIED WALNUTS 20

TOASTED, SALTED PISTACHIO NUTS 21

PEACH LEAF WINE 22

SECCO'S FLAKY TOMATO
AND OLIVE TART 23

ASIAN MIXED NUTS
WITH KAFFIR LIME DUST 27

MINIATURE ONION AND
GOAT CHEESE *TATINS* 28

ROSEMARY-INFUSED ALMONDS
WITH HOMEMADE ALMOND OIL 30

CHEESE STRAWS WITH PARMESAN,
SHEEP'S MILK CHEESE, AND
ESPELETTE PEPPER 32

HAM AND CHEESE SQUARES WITH CORNICHONS

~ Makes 18 squares, to serve 6 to 8 ~

Is there a better palate opener than a single bite of a grilled ham and cheese sand-wich, brightened by the tart crunch of a cornichon? Assemble all the ingredients for these baby *croque monsieur* sandwiches earlier in the day, and then prepare them at the last minute when guests and family are gathering.

EQUIPMENT: A toaster; a nonstick skillet; toothpicks.

4 slices Saffron and Honey Brioche (page 228) or white bread (*pain de mie*), crusts removed

2 teaspoons French mustard

2 thin slices best-quality cooked ham, cut to fit 2 slices of the bread

About 1/4 cup (30 g) freshly grated Swiss Gruyère cheese or other hard cheese

1 tablespoon (15 g) Clarified Butter (page 291) or unsalted butter

9 cornichons, halved lengthwise

1. Toast the brioche or bread. Coat one side of each slice with the mustard. Place a slice of ham over the mustard on two of the slices. Sprinkle the cheese over the ham. Place the other slices of bread, mustard-coated side down, on top of the cheese.

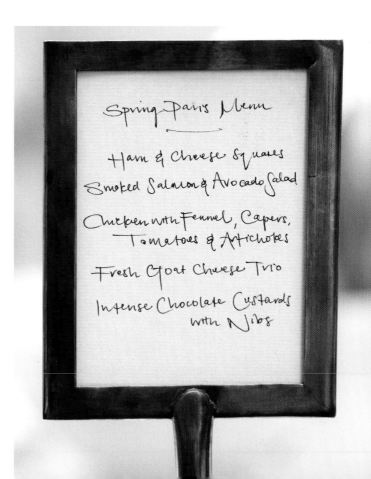

Spring Paris Menu

Ham & Cheese Squares
Smoked Salmon & Avocado Salad
Chicken with Fennel, Capers,
    Tomatoes & Artichokes
Fresh Goat Cheese Trio
Intense Chocolate Custards
    with Nibs

2. In the skillet, melt the butter over low heat. Brown the bread evenly on both sides, about
    1 minute per side. Cut each sandwich into 9 even squares. Pierce each cornichon half with a
    toothpick and secure the toothpick to the grilled bread. Arrange on a serving platter and serve
    warm, offering guests cocktail napkins.

WINE SUGGESTION: Grilled cheese and champagne? Why not? I love Pierre
Moncuit's *blanc de blancs*, a medium-bodied, clean, and always reliable offering that
has a purity that matches just about any opening taste.

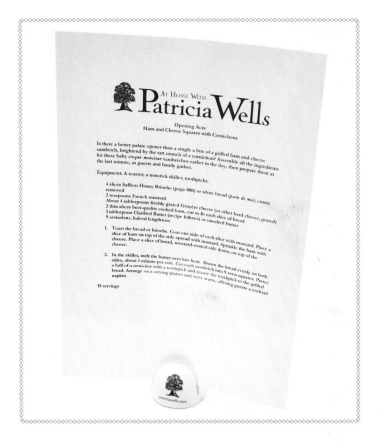

Whether testing or re-testing recipes, I always have a written recipe at hand, to consult,
correct, embellish. Years ago I found a good solution to keeping them off the counter: these
wonderful Page-Ups (originally designed for working at a computer with printed copy)
hold the recipe upright and (mostly) out of harm's way.

ONION AND GRUYÈRE BITES

~ Makes 16 bites ~

Think of these delicate bites as French onion soup on a tasty slice of sourdough or buttery brioche. The preparation is open to many variations: add herbs, such as rosemary or sage; add mushrooms, such as button mushrooms or morels; or of course add truffle butter and thin slices of fresh black truffle. The cheese can also be varied: any grated hard cheese works well here, including the peppery Pecorino Romano and the rich French Basque sheep's milk cheese *brebis*. For a large party, try many variations so guests can choose their flavor of the night! For a rustic presentation, prepare this on a whole slice of toasted sourdough bread. For a more elegant approach, toast bread or brioche and cut the slices into small rounds.

EQUIPMENT: A steamer; a toaster; a 2 1/2-inch (6 1/2 cm) round
biscuit cutter; a baking sheet lined with baking parchment.

2 medium (about 8 ounces; 250 g) sweet white onions, peeled and cut crosswise into thin rings

2 to 3 slices Saffron and Honey Brioche (page 228) or sourdough bread

1 to 2 tablespoons (15 to 30 g) unsalted butter

Fine sea salt

Coarse, freshly ground black pepper

1 teaspoon fresh lemon thyme or regular thyme leaves (or minced rosemary or sage)

About 1/2 cup (60 g) freshly grated Swiss Gruyère cheese or other hard cheese

1. Bring 1 quart (1 l) of water to a simmer in the bottom of the steamer. Place the onions on the steaming rack. Place the rack over the simmering water, cover, and steam until the onions are "al dente," about 5 minutes. Transfer the onions to a bowl. (The onions can be prepared up to

8 hours in advance. Store in an airtight container in the refrigerator. Bring to room temperature at serving time.)

2. Arrange a rack in the oven about 3 inches (7.5 cm) from the heat source. Preheat the broiler.

3. Toast the brioche or bread. With the biscuit cutter, cut the toast into 16 rounds. Spread the rounds lightly with butter. Arrange the rounds side by side on the baking sheet.

4. Season the onions lightly with salt and generously with pepper. Spoon a tablespoon of the onions on top of the butter on each toast round. Sprinkle with the thyme and grated cheese.

5. Place the baking sheet under the broiler and broil just until the cheese melts, about 1 minute. Serve immediately.

SAUTÉED DATES WITH FENNEL AND WALNUTS

~ Makes 24 dates ~

Dried fruits are used freely in our cooking classes, and this is a new variation on an all-time favorite, dates stuffed with almonds. Here walnuts and fennel offer a richness and a pleasant crunch, a nice contrast to the smooth, sweet, and supple dates. Be sure to inform guests that the pit has been removed from the date, or the walnut filling may be rejected! I prefer large, naturally sweet Medjool dates, always a healthy treat.

EQUIPMENT: Toothpicks, for serving.

24 whole Medjool dates

1 teaspoon fennel seeds

24 walnut halves

2 teaspoons extra-virgin olive oil

Coarse, freshly ground black pepper

Fleur de sel or fine sea salt

1. Pit a date but do not cut all the way through. Sprinkle the inside of the date with a few fennel seeds and stuff it with a walnut. Press the date closed. Repeat with the remaining dates.

2. Heat the oil in a frying pan over moderate heat. Add the dates and brown them very lightly, 2 to 3 minutes. Remove from the heat, season with pepper and salt, and transfer to a serving platter. Place a toothpick in each date. Serve warm, offering guests cocktail napkins.

ANCHOVY BITES

~ Makes 75 pastries, to serve 25 to 30 ~

Students love to make these savory, quick, easy, and satisfying opening acts. Home-made Anchovy Cream is simply spread on top of homemade or prepared puff pastry; the pastry is cut into bite-size rounds, then baked until golden. These are best warm from the oven, but they are also delicious at room temperature or rewarmed at serving time in a low oven. This is a real nothing-goes-to-waste recipe: the "skeleton" of prepared pastry left after cutting out the rounds can be baked until crisp, then broken into shards to shower over salads or soups or to serve simply as a snack.

EQUIPMENT: A 1 1/2-inch (3 cm) round biscuit cutter;
2 baking sheets lined with baking parchment.

1 recipe Anchovy Cream (page 19)

A 14-ounce (400 g) sheet of Blitz Puff Pastry (page 294) or purchased all-butter puff pastry, thawed (see Note)

1. Evenly center two racks in the oven. Preheat the oven to 375°F (190°C).

2. Spread the Anchovy Cream evenly over the entire sheet of pastry, going right out to the edges. With the biscuit cutter, cut out about 75 rounds of pastry. (Note: You will get the most from the pastry if you begin on the outside and cut rings as tightly as possible from the outside. Then work from the next large inside ring.) Arrange the rounds side by side on one of the baking sheets.

3. Carefully transfer the remaining "skeleton" of dressed pastry to the second baking sheet. Place the baking sheets in the oven and bake until the pastry is puffed and golden, about 10 minutes. Remove from the oven. Serve the appetizer rounds warm or at room temperature. The rounds

and the "skeleton" shards can be stored in an airtight container at room temperature for up to 2 days.

NOTE: In our tests, we have preferred Dufour brand frozen puff pastry, available at most specialty supermarkets. See www.dufourpastrykitchens.com. Be sure to leave ample time for thawing frozen dough, at least 6 hours in the refrigerator.

ANCHOVY CREAM

~ Makes 1/2 cup (125 ml) ~

Each day in cooking class we prepare at least one or two appetizers, a sign that it's time to open a bottle of wine and relax. And this is a perennial favorite. Throughout Provence *anchoïade* (anchovy cream) is a popular starter, often used as a dip for a selection of raw vegetables. Recipes vary dramatically from cook to cook and I like to keep mine simple, with just a trio of ingredients: top-quality anchovy fillets cured in olive oil, capers, and cream.

EQUIPMENT: A mini food processor or a standard food processor fitted with a small bowl.

One 2.82-ounce (80 g) jar Italian anchovy fillets in olive oil (about 20 fillets)

1 tablespoon capers in vinegar, drained

1/4 cup (60 ml) light cream or half-and-half

Combine the ingredients in the bowl of the food processor and process to a chunky consistency. Use as a dip for raw vegetables, to prepare Anchovy Bites (page 16), or as a sandwich spread. (Store in an airtight container in the refrigerator for up to 3 days.)

CURRIED WALNUTS

~ Makes 2 cups (250 g) ~

These appetizer nuts are in the list of Top 10 tastes we love to begin a party or a meal. Homemade Curry Powder and of course really fresh walnuts are The Secret.

EQUIPMENT: A baking sheet.

◇◇◇

2 cups (250 g) walnut halves

1 tablespoon tamari or other Japanese soy sauce, preferably organic

2 teaspoons Homemade Curry Powder (page 282)

◇◇◇

1. Center a rack in the oven. Preheat the oven to 350°F (175°C).

2. In a bowl, combine the walnuts and tamari, tossing to coat the nuts evenly. Add the curry powder and toss once more.

3. Spread the nuts in a single layer on the baking sheet. Place in the oven and bake, shaking the sheet from time to time, until the nuts are fragrantly toasted, 8 to 10 minutes. Remove from the oven and transfer the nuts to a dish to cool. (Store in an airtight container at room temperature for up to 1 week.)

TOASTED, SALTED PISTACHIO NUTS

~ Makes 1 cup (125 g) ~

These toasted pistachio nuts make a great snack, and can always be found in our pantry.

---

1 cup (125 g) raw, unsalted shelled pistachio nuts

1 teaspoon best-quality pistachio oil, such as Leblanc brand, or extra-virgin olive oil

1/4 teaspoon fine sea salt

In a small skillet, combine the pistachios, oil, and salt and toss to blend. Cook over moderate heat, shaking the pan regularly, until the nuts are fragrant, evenly toasted, and beginning to crackle and sizzle, 3 to 4 minutes. Watch carefully! They can burn quickly. Transfer the nuts to a large plate to cool. (Store in an airtight container at room temperature for up to 1 week.)

PEACH LEAF WINE

~ Makes 1 1/2 quarts (1.5 l) ~

Who could imagine a simple peach leaf could give up so much flavor? When infused, peach leaves give off an almond-like essence, and here in combination with cinnamon and cloves, one arrives at a fragrant, refreshing aperitif. If you don't have a peach tree in your backyard, ask at the farmer's market and a merchant might save some for you.

EQUIPMENT: A glass jar with a lid; 3 clean, empty wine bottles, with corks.

120 peach leaves, preferably organic and unsprayed, washed and dried

1 cinnamon stick

4 whole cloves

2 bottles (1.5 l) dry white wine

1 cup (200 g) sugar

1 cup (250 ml) vodka

1. In the glass jar, combine the peach leaves, spices, and wine. Stir to mix. Cover and set aside at room temperature for 4 days.

2. Strain, discarding the leaves and spices. Add the sugar and vodka. Stir to dissolve the sugar. Cover and set aside at room temperature for 10 days.

3. Transfer the wine to the wine bottles. Cork the bottles. Store in the refrigerator for up to 3 months. Serve chilled.

SECCO'S FLAKY TOMATO AND OLIVE TART

~ 8 servings ~

Secco is an alluring, all-purpose *boulangerie* and *pâtisserie* in Paris's chic 6th arrondissement. I could easily visit the shop every day to sample a giant slice of this
unforgettably delicious tomato tart. We prepare this in most cooking classes, always
to raves.

EQUIPMENT: A baking sheet lined with baking parchment.

An 8-ounce (250 g) sheet of Blitz Puff Pastry (page 294) or purchased all-butter puff pastry, thawed
(see Note)

1/4 cup (25 g) freshly grated Parmigiano-Reggiano cheese

12 ounces (750 g) tomatoes, cored and cut crosswise into thin slices

Fine sea salt

2 ounces (60 g) shavings of Parmigiano-Reggiano cheese

25 best-quality black olives, pitted

A small handful of fresh basil leaves, left whole

Small handful of fresh oregano

Hot red pepper flakes, for serving

1. Unroll the pastry, place it on the baking sheet, and prick it all over with a fork. Shower with the
   grated cheese. Freeze for 30 minutes.

2. Center a rack in the oven. Preheat the oven to 400°F (200°C).

3. Arrange the tomato slices side by side on a thick layer of paper towels. Season them generously with salt. Set aside for 10 minutes. (This will draw out excess liquid from the tomatoes and help prevent the tart from becoming soggy.)

4. Remove the baking sheet from the freezer, place it in the oven, and prebake for 5 minutes. Remove from the oven. If the pastry has puffed, prick it with a fork to deflate it. Arrange the tomatoes in a slightly overlapping layer on top of the pastry. Shower with the cheese shavings and the black olives. Return to the oven and bake until the pastry is a deep golden, the tomatoes are soft, and the cheese has melted, about 20 minutes. Shower with the basil and oregano while still hot from the oven. Serve warm or at room temperature, cut into 8 equal wedges. Pass hot pepper flakes for additional seasoning.

THE SECRET: Prebaking the pastry with a light coating of cheese makes for a more full-flavored, firm tart. Placing the dough on a parchment-lined baking sheet will prevent it from sticking to the baking sheet.

NOTE: In our tests, we have preferred Dufour brand frozen puff pastry, available at most specialty supermarkets. See www.dufourpastrykitchens.com. Be sure to leave ample time for thawing frozen dough, at least 6 hours in the refrigerator.

ASIAN MIXED NUTS WITH KAFFIR LIME DUST

~ Makes 3 cups (340 g) ~

I am always on the lookout for unusual appetizers, and this one brings back memories of travels to Vietnam, where kaffir lime and all varieties of nuts—especially peanuts—appear freely and frequently. Kaffir lime trees grow easily, so if you live in a temperate climate, add one to your garden or patio. Fresh, frozen, and dried leaves can be found at Asian food shops. Fresh leaves, of course, are the most intensely flavored.

EQUIPMENT: A baking sheet.

1 1/2 cups (170 g) dry-roasted salted peanuts

1 1/2 cups (170 g) dry-roasted salted cashews

Extra-virgin olive oil spray

12 fresh, frozen, or dried kaffir lime leaves, chopped, then ground to a fine powder (2 teaspoons, see Note)

1. Center a rack in the oven. Preheat the oven to 350°F (175°C).

2. Combine the nuts on the baking sheet. Spray them lightly with oil and toss to coat.

3. Place the baking sheet in the oven and lightly toast the nuts, 8 to 10 minutes, tossing them occasionally.

4. Transfer the nuts to a bowl, and while still warm, toss with the kaffir lime dust. (Store in an airtight container at room temperature for up to 1 week.)

NOTE: Dried kaffir lime leaves can be found in Patricia's Pantry at my Amazon Store, accessed via the home page of www.PatriciaWells.com.

MINIATURE ONION AND GOAT CHEESE *TATINS*

~ Makes 24 miniature *tatins* ~

These tasty, savory, miniature pastries are a huge hit in my cooking classes. There is always a great sense of satisfaction when one removes a tray of these fragrant, golden nuggets from the oven. These are best warm from the oven but are also delicious at room temperature. They can serve as appetizers or as sides to a simple green salad.

EQUIPMENT: A 2 3/4-inch (7 cm) round biscuit cutter; 2 baking sheets lined with baking parchment; a food processor; 2 nonstick *petit four* molds or mini muffin tins, each with twelve 2 1/2-inch (6.5 cm) cups, or a 24-cup mini-muffin pan.

A 14-ounce (400 g) sheet of Blitz Puff Pastry (page 294) or purchased all-butter puff pastry, thawed (see Note)

4 tablespoons (60 g) unsalted butter

1 pound (500 g) onions, peeled, halved lengthwise, and cut into thin half-moons

Fine sea salt

Coarse, freshly ground black pepper

4 ounces (125 g) soft fresh goat's milk cheese

Grated zest of 1 lemon, preferably organic

3 large eggs, preferably organic and free-range, lightly beaten

1 teaspoon fresh lemon thyme or regular thyme leaves

Fleur de sel, for garnish

1.   Evenly center two racks in the oven. Preheat the oven to 400°F (200°C).

2. With the biscuit cutter, cut out 24 rounds of pastry. (Note: you will get the most from the pastry if you begin on the outside and cut rings as tightly as possible from the outside. Then work from the next large inside ring. I usually get 31 rounds out of a sheet.) Arrange the rounds side by side on the baking sheets. Prick them with a fork and freeze for at least 10 minutes.

3. In a skillet, melt the butter over low heat. Add the onions and a pinch of salt, and sweat—cook, covered, over low heat until soft and translucent—about 10 minutes. Season with pepper.

4. In the food processor, combine the goat cheese, lemon zest, eggs, and half of the thyme leaves and process to blend. Add the cheese mixture to the onions in the skillet and stir to blend. Taste for seasoning.

5. Spoon a tablespoon of the mixture into each mold or muffin cup. Cover each one with a round of pastry.

6. Place the molds or tins in the oven and bake until the pastry is puffed and golden, about 25 minutes. Remove from the oven and let cool slightly. Then remove them from the cups and turn them over, pastry side down. Serve warm or at room temperature, garnished with the remaining thyme leaves and *fleur de sel*.

WINE SUGGESTION: The mineral-rich flavors of a blend of Marsanne, Clairette, Ugni Blanc, and Bourboulenc with their touch of spice make Domaine du Paternel Cassis Blanc de Blancs a perfect palate opener to pair with the *tatins*.

THE SECRET: Make sure that you cut the pastry slightly larger than the diameter of the molds, since the pastry may shrink in baking.

VARIATIONS: Replace the goat cheese with grated cheddar and bits of bacon; Feta cheese; crabmeat and tarragon; or peas, scallions, and pancetta. Add herbs. Bake as simple, lighter, "quiche-like" bites without the pastry.

NOTE: In our tests, we have preferred Dufour brand frozen puff pastry, available at most specialty supermarkets. See www.dufourpastrykitchens.com. Be sure to leave ample time for thawing frozen dough, at least 6 hours in the refrigerator.

ROSEMARY-INFUSED ALMONDS WITH HOMEMADE ALMOND OIL

~ Makes 2 cups (360 g) ~

While I was preparing a cooking demonstration for the Google staff in San Francisco, the chef presented me with the most delicious homemade pistachio oil. He said he couldn't readily find what I had requested in the local market, so he prepared a batch himself! That put me in a creative mood, and now when the proper nut oil is not readily at hand, I make my own. Here's a version I created using almonds. I use the oil to embellish all manner of foods, from braised asparagus to these toasted, herb-infused almonds.

EQUIPMENT: A small, nonstick skillet; an electric spice mill; a baking sheet.

2 1/2 cups (360 g) top-quality whole unblanched almonds

1/3 cup (75 ml) neutral vegetable oil, such as grapeseed, peanut, or safflower

1 tablespoon minced fresh rosemary, plus 4 fresh rosemary sprigs

1/2 teaspoon grated lemon zest, preferably organic

1/2 teaspoon fine sea salt

Fresh rosemary sprigs, for serving

1. Prepare the almond oil: In the skillet, toast 1/2 cup (60 g) of the almonds over moderate heat, tossing from time to time to toast them evenly, until toasty and fragrant, about 5 minutes. Remove to a plate to cool. Once cooled, transfer the nuts to the spice mill and grind coarsely, to about the size of a small grain of rice.

2. In a small saucepan, warm the vegetable oil. Off the heat, add the ground almonds and stir to blend. Set aside for at least 1 hour to infuse the oil. Then transfer the oil and nuts to an airtight container and store in the refrigerator for up to 3 days.

3. Center a rack in the oven. Preheat the oven to 350°F (175°C).

4. In a large bowl, combine the remaining 2 cups (300 g) almonds, 1 tablespoon of the almond oil (with the ground nuts), the minced rosemary, the lemon zest, and the salt. Toss to coat the nuts. Transfer to the baking sheet. Scatter the 4 rosemary sprigs on top.

5. Place the baking sheet in the oven and toast until the almonds are fragrant and golden, about 5 minutes. Transfer to a bowl and let cool. Once cooled, remove and discard the rosemary sprigs. (Store in an airtight container at room temperature for up to 1 week.) At serving time, garnish with fresh rosemary sprigs.

CHEESE STRAWS WITH PARMESAN, SHEEP'S MILK CHEESE, AND *ESPELETTE* PEPPER

~ Makes about 20 cheese straws ~

When either I or my students are in for a bit of a challenge—as well as the satisfaction of turning out fragrant, crunchy appetizer treats—we bake these beautiful puff pastry cheese straws that look as though they belong in the tempting window of a very fancy pastry shop.

EQUIPMENT: 4 baking sheets lined with baking parchment.

1/2 cup (50 g) freshly grated Parmigiano-Reggiano cheese

1/2 cup (35 g) freshly grated sheep's milk cheese, such as Pecorino

1 teaspoon ground *Espelette* pepper or other mild chile pepper

1/2 teaspoon fine sea salt

A 14-ounce (400 g) sheet of Blitz Puff Pastry (page 294), or purchased all-butter puff pastry, thawed (see Note)

1 large egg, preferably organic and free-range

1. In a bowl, combine the cheeses, pepper, and salt.

2. On a well-floured work surface—a marble pastry slab or wooden cutting board—roll the pastry into a 10-inch (25 cm) square. Flour as needed to prevent the dough from sticking to the work surface: the pastry should move freely as you roll it. Place the pastry on one of the parchment-lined baking sheets and refrigerate for 20 minutes.

3. In a bowl, prepare an egg wash by whisking together the egg and 1 tablespoon of room temperature water.

4. Cut a piece of baking parchment 20 inches (50 cm) long. Lay the parchment on the work surface. Sprinkle half of the cheese mixture to cover a 15 x 10-inch (32.5 x 25 cm) area of the parchment. Remove the pastry from the refrigerator. Brush one side with the egg wash. Carefully transfer the puff pastry, egg wash side down, onto the cheese-lined parchment. Brush the second side with the egg wash. Evenly sprinkle the remaining cheese over the puff pastry. With the rolling pin, carefully roll over the puff pastry, pressing gently so the cheese adheres to the surface of the pastry.

5. With a pizza cutter, cut the puff pastry into strips about 1/2 inch (1.25 cm) wide and 15 inches (32.5 cm) long. Working quickly, carefully move 5 or 6 pastry strips to each of the parchment-lined baking sheets, making sure you leave room between the strips to allow for expansion when baking. With your fingertips, grab each end of a strip and twist it like a corkscrew. Continue until all the strips have been twisted. Place the baking sheets in the refrigerator for 20 minutes.

6. Evenly center two racks in the oven. Preheat the oven to 375°F (190°C).

7. Remove the baking sheets from the refrigerator, place them in the oven, and bake until the cheese straws are golden and puffed, 25 to 30 minutes. (This may have to be done in batches.) Remove the baking sheets to a rack. Serve warm or at room temperature. (Store in an airtight container at room temperature for up to 3 days.)

NOTES:

• In our tests, we have preferred Dufour brand frozen puff pastry, available at most specialty supermarkets. See www.dufourpastrykitchens.com. Be sure to leave ample time for thawing frozen dough, at least 6 hours in the refrigerator.

• *Espelette* pepper can be found in Patricia's Pantry at my Amazon Store, accessed via the home page of www.PatriciaWells.com.

A TREASURE FROM A MENTOR

After Julia's stove had a major overhaul, I had kitchen towels monogrammed in her honor and memory.

One of the most amazing things about Julia Child was her total straightforwardness. Once, years ago, when I was saddened by a mutual friend's passing, she responded, matter-of-factly: "But he led a good, long life." And so did she.

Julia was my mentor, friend, a model for how to conduct one's life. It was totally humbling that my first encounter with this *grande dame* was a fan letter she wrote in 1984 upon publication of my first book, *The Food Lover's Guide to Paris.*

We met face to face shortly afterward, and for a good decade, nearly every time she came to France, we would get together. The quips and stories never stopped. Once she and a younger friend flew from California to Paris and immediately boarded the TGV to Provence. As she looked out the window watching the porter-less travelers struggling with their bags, she said to my friend, "I wonder what old people do." She was well past eighty at the time!

She and her husband, Paul, helped celebrate my fortieth birthday at Chanteduc, and a few years later we honored Julia's eightieth with a

After acquiring Julia's stove, we installed it in a small room off our center courtyard and just inside the outdoor bread oven. To the left is the entrance to our treasured wine cellar.

dancing party on the terrace, complete with live music from a Barbary organ. One year we were panelists at a Young Presidents' Organization meeting in Cannes. After the first day she called me on the phone and said, "This is sort of like a Shriners' convention. Let's get out of here and go to a good restaurant."

That evening, we had a magical dinner at Restaurant de Bacon in Cap d'Antibes, a place I knew well. Julia loved all the attention that was showered on us, and begged to go the next night "to a place where they know you."

That was also the time she instructed me to dye my hair. It had become a mousy brown with streaks of curly gray, but I was too much of a good Catholic girl to consider anointing my hair with scandalous dye. Julia just looked at me and said, simply, "People say you look younger if you don't dye your hair. Well, they're just wrong!" The next week I made an appointment at Carita in Paris, and I have never looked back.

But the best part of the story is Julia's stove. When Julia lived in Grasse in the 1960s, she outfitted her kitchen with a La Cornue stove, a shiny

Here we see Julia's kitchen in Provence, where her La Cornue was first installed.
Note the pegboards used to hang pots and pans and utensils, Julia's signature!

white Art Deco—style model. In 1991, she stayed with us at Thanksgiving, on her way to close down the summer house for good. I asked if I could buy her stove. (For me, it was the equivalent of having Freud's couch.) She said no. But the next morning she came down to breakfast and said she'd changed her mind. I could have the stove.

We created a cool summer kitchen with a stone floor, a marble sink, and Julia's stove, a cantankerous two-burner gas treasure with an oven that seems to have only one temperature, really hot, no matter how you set it. In the summer I have a quiet ritual: I light the stove each morning, then head for the vegetable garden to gather what has to be picked that day and what might be roasted in the oven. I go to the gym and by the time I am finished, many of the basics for lunch and dinner have been made.

Shortly before Julia died, I e-mailed her to thank her again for the stove and deliver news of her trusty La Cornue. As usual, she e-mailed back within seconds, saying she only wished she could be here and cook on that stove once more.

For years I saved mementos of her visits: pictures, menus we've all signed, songs that students have written after cooking in Julia's Kitchen. One day I decided to frame those pictures and mementos and hang them in Julia's Kitchen—I was nostalgic and felt her presence more than ever. Later that day I got the call about her death. Sweet Julia did indeed live a good, long life.

Visiting friends, weekend guests, line up for a group photo in 1992.

For many years running in the 1980s and '90s, Julia and I were on the program at the June Food & Wine magazine event in Aspen, Colorado. Here we are lunching with Paul Johnson, a friend and local chef who helped with my cooking demonstrations.

When my new kitchen was completed in 1992, we celebrated with a weekend of feasting with friends.

SALADS

FETA AND WATERMELON SALAD
WITH MINT AND BABY GREENS 43

SMOKED SALMON AND AVOCADO SALAD
WITH GINGER-LEMON DRESSING 45

TOMATO AND MOZZARELLA STACKS
ON A BED OF BASIL 47

PEAR, FENNEL, BELGIAN ENDIVE,
AND CURRIED WALNUT SALAD 48

MONDAY NIGHT BEEF SALAD
WITH GREEN BEANS, AVOCADO,
AND ARUGULA 51

ASIAN COLESLAW WITH
SESAME SOY DRESSING 53

HEIRLOOM TOMATO PLATTER
WITH HERBS AND CHEESE 54

WATERCRESS AND MINT SALAD
WITH PEANUTS 56

MINI PALAIS'S *BURRATA*
AND HAM SALAD 57

BETSY'S COLD VIETNAMESE
SHRIMP AND NOODLE SALAD 59

CHAR-GRILLED EGGPLANT
SALAD WITH FRESH MINT 62

FETA AND WATERMELON SALAD WITH MINT AND BABY GREENS

~ 4 servings ~

Okay, this salad wins the beauty award, hands down! When guests spy this huge slice of brilliant red, dewy watermelon, view the pristine white of the Feta cheese, and take a whiff of the fresh mint chiffonade and the baby greens, they are ready to dig in. Serve it with a few slices of toasted country bread and you have a perfect, light salad as a meal. I like to slice the watermelon into a thick round, but it can also be cut into chunks.

EQUIPMENT: 4 chilled dinner plates.

About 2 pounds (1 kg) watermelon, rind removed (about 8 ounces; 250 g per person)

1 cup (125 g) crumbled Greek Feta cheese

1 cup (35 g) fresh mint leaves, cut into a chiffonade

About 1 cup (125 g) lentil sprouts, microgreens, or baby greens

Lemon–Olive Oil Dressing (recipe follows) or dressing of choice

If you are serving the watermelon in rounds, cut it about 1 inch (2.5 cm) thick and 5 inches (12.5 cm) around. Place a round on each of the dinner plates. Scatter the Feta, mint, and sprouts over each melon round and drizzle with the dressing.

WINE SUGGESTION: A white with personality is in order here. I am in love with the wines from the Châteauneuf-du-Pape estate Domaine de la Vieille Julienne. They offer a delicious white *vin de table*, a lightly floral, frank, and forward blend of Grenache Blanc, Bourboulenc, Clairette, and Marsanne, a fine pairing for the Feta, mint, and melon.

LEMON—OLIVE OIL DRESSING

~ Makes about 1 1/4 cups (310 ml) ~

EQUIPMENT: A small jar with a lid.

1/4 cup (60 ml) freshly squeezed lemon juice

Fine sea salt

1 cup (250 ml) extra-virgin olive oil

Place the lemon juice and salt in the jar. Cover and shake to dissolve the salt. Add the oil and shake to blend. Taste for seasoning. (Store in the refrigerator for up to 1 week.) Shake again at serving time to create a thick emulsion.

Garlic flowers make a perfect garnish for salads or soups.

SMOKED SALMON AND AVOCADO SALAD WITH GINGER-LEMON DRESSING

~ 4 servings ~

There are some ingredients I never get enough of, and smoked salmon, avocado, and ginger are three of them. This perky salad is great any time of year—a pretty pastel palette of pink, yellow, and green.

EQUIPMENT: A small jar with a lid; 4 chilled dinner plates.

2 tablespoons freshly squeezed lemon juice

Grated zest of 2 lemons preferably organic

2 tablespoons grated fresh ginger

1/4 teaspoon fine sea salt

1/3 cup (90 ml) extra-virgin olive oil

8 thin slices (about 8 ounces; 250 g) smoked salmon

2 large ripe avocados, halved, pitted, peeled, and cut lengthwise into thin slices

Coarse, freshly ground black pepper

4 fresh dill sprigs (optional)

Lemon wedges, for garnish (optional)

1. In the jar, combine the lemon juice, zest, grated ginger, and salt. Cover the jar and shake to blend. Add the oil, cover the jar, and shake to blend. Taste for seasoning.

2. Arrange 2 slices of salmon on each dinner plate. Drizzle with a bit of the dressing. Fan out half of an avocado on top of each serving of salmon. Drizzle with a bit of the dressing. Season with pepper. If using, garnish each plate with fresh dill and lemon wedges. Serve.

WINE SUGGESTION: The smoke, mineral, and spice from A. et P. de Villaine's Bourgogne Aligoté de Bouzeron—a dry white Burgundy from the Aligoté grape—makes this an ideal match for salmon and avocado.

TOMATO AND MOZZARELLA STACKS ON A BED OF BASIL

~ 4 servings ~

When the summer garden is in full swing, this lunch salad appears often, always with intense pleasure! I like to use the medium-size Evergreen or Green Zebra tomatoes, but any top-quality tomato, of any color, will do.

EQUIPMENT: Four 5-inch (12.5 cm) bamboo picks.

4 Evergreen tomatoes (each about 3 ounces; 90 g)

About 5 ounces (150 g) Italian buffalo-milk Mozzarella cheese

16 fresh basil leaves, torn

Extra-virgin olive oil spray

Fleur de sel

There's no use slicing a tomato with a dull knife.

For each serving, core a tomato and slice it into 4 crosswise slices. Cut the Mozzarella to the same thickness and layer 3 pieces of cheese between the 4 slices of tomato. Secure with a bamboo pick and set on a bed of basil. Spray with a touch of oil and season with salt.

PEAR, FENNEL, BELGIAN ENDIVE, AND CURRIED WALNUT SALAD

~ 4 servings ~

Eyes light up when this salad appears at the table, a cold-weather treat full of crunch, color, and flavor. The dressing can be prepared in advance and refrigerated.

EQUIPMENT: A small jar with a lid; 4 chilled salad plates.

Walnut Dressing

1 shallot, peeled and finely minced

3 tablespoons best-quality walnut or hazelnut oil, such as Leblanc brand

1 tablespoon brown rice vinegar, preferably organic

1/2 teaspoon fine sea salt

2 large, firm pears, cored, sliced, and cut into matchsticks (do not peel)

2 small fennel bulbs, trimmed and cut lengthwise into matchsticks

1 Belgian endive head, trimmed and cut lengthwise into matchsticks

1 cup (125 g) Curried Walnuts (page 20)

4 tablespoons minced fresh chives

1. In the small jar, combine the shallot, oil, rice vinegar, and salt. Cover and shake to blend. Taste for seasoning.

2. In a large salad bowl, combine the pears, fennel, and endive. Toss with just enough dressing to coat them lightly and evenly. Taste for seasoning. Serve on the salad plates, garnished with the walnuts and chives.

Stack, stack, stack! Even in the largest of kitchens, economy of space is important. When shopping
for any kitchen objects, I favor stacking bowls, cups, and utensils every time.

MONDAY NIGHT BEEF SALAD WITH GREEN BEANS, AVOCADO, AND ARUGULA

~ 4 servings ~

My husband, Walter, often cooks his famed Salt and Pepper Steak (page 111) on Sunday nights, and we always hope for enough leftovers to prepare this salad as a meal the following day.

EQUIPMENT: A small jar with a lid; a 5-quart (5 l) pasta pot fitted with a colander.

Dressing

2 tablespoons minced fresh tarragon leaves

2 teaspoons tarragon-flavored mustard (see Note)

2 tablespoons freshly squeezed lemon juice

1/2 cup (125 ml) extra-virgin olive oil

2 tablespoons capers in vinegar, drained

6 cornichons, cut crosswise into thin rings

3 tablespoons coarse sea salt

8 ounces (250 g) green beans

10 ounces (300 g) cooked beef rib steak, cubed

4 scallions, white and green parts peeled and cut into thin rings

A large handful (60 g) arugula, rinsed and dried

10 firm cherry tomatoes, halved lengthwise

1 large ripe avocado, halved, pitted, peeled, and cubed

1. In the jar, combine all the dressing ingredients. Cover and shake to blend. Taste for seasoning.

2. Fill the pasta pot with 3 quarts (3 l) of water and bring to a rolling boil over high heat. Prepare a bowl of ice water for an ice bath.

3. Add the coarse salt and the beans to the boiling water and blanch until crisp-tender, 3 to 4 minutes. (The cooking time will vary according to the size and tenderness of the beans.) Immediately remove the colander from the water, allow the water to drain from the beans, and plunge the beans into the ice water so they cool down as quickly as possible. (The beans will cool in 1 to 2 minutes. If you leave them longer, they will become soggy and begin to lose flavor.) Drain the beans and wrap them in a thick towel to dry. (The beans can be cooked up to 4 hours in advance. Keep them wrapped in the towel and refrigerate, if desired.)

4. Place the beef in a large bowl. Add just enough dressing to lightly coat the meat. Toss to blend. Add the beans and scallions, and add just enough dressing to lightly coat the ingredients. Tear the arugula into bite-size pieces. Add the arugula, tomatoes, and avocado to the bowl, and add just enough dressing to lightly coat the ingredients. Taste for seasoning. Serve.

NOTE: I favor Edmond Fallot's Tarragon Dijon Mustard, which can be found in Patricia's Pantry at my Amazon Store, accessed via the home page of www.PatriciaWells.com.

ASIAN COLESLAW WITH SESAME SOY DRESSING

~ 4 servings ~

Since childhood, coleslaw has been one of my favorite salads. Here it acquires an Asian accent, anointed with a mix of sesame, soy sauce, and a touch of freshly grated ginger.

EQUIPMENT: A small jar with a lid.

Dressing

2 tablespoons best-quality toasted sesame oil, such as Leblanc brand

2 tablespoons brown rice vinegar, preferably organic

1 tablespoon soy sauce, preferably organic

1 teaspoon grated fresh ginger

1/4 small cabbage, finely shredded

1 large carrot, peeled and grated

1. In the small jar, combine all the ingredients for the dressing. Cover and shake to blend. Taste for seasoning.

2. In a large bowl, combine the cabbage and carrot and toss to blend. Add the dressing and toss once more. Taste for seasoning. Serve.

HEIRLOOM TOMATO PLATTER WITH HERBS AND CHEESE

~ 6 servings ~

When my garden is at its peak in the summer months, we can't get enough of the multicolored heirloom tomatoes. This is a favorite salad preparation, combining red and orange-toned tomatoes cut crosswise, then garnished with an avalanche of garden herbs and various cheeses. Here we top the tomatoes and greens with ruffles of the firm Swiss Tête de Moine, shaved with a special machine called a *girolle*, but any cheese of choice can be used here.

EQUIPMENT: A cheese *girolle*, a mandoline, or a very sharp knife; a large serving platter.

6 ripe heirloom tomatoes (about 1 1/4 pounds; 625 g), preferably of varied colors

6 thin ruffles of Tête de Moine cheese, created with a *girolle* if available (see Note)

A handful of varied fresh herbs, such as green basil, purple basil, *shiso*, and/or Delfino cilantro

About 2 tablespoons Lemon–Olive Oil Dressing (page 44)

Fleur de sel

Arrange the tomatoes in overlapping layers on the serving platter. Garnish with the cheese and herbs. Drizzle the dressing over all and season lightly with *fleur de sel*.

NOTE: A cheese *girolle* can be found in Items for a Dream Kitchen at my Amazon Store, accessed via the home page of www.PatriciaWells.com. If you do not have a *girolle*, cut the cheese into paper-thin slices with a mandoline or a very sharp knife.

From July to October, multiple varieties of heirloom tomatoes in our vegetable garden offer us a steady supply of treats.

Oregano, with its tiny yet pungent leaves, has become a recent favorite in my garden. In season I shower it on everything, from a simple tossed green salad, to a tomato platter, to soups.

WATERCRESS AND MINT SALAD WITH PEANUTS

~ 4 to 6 servings ~

This was a rave salad during our weeklong cooking class in Vietnam, and it remains part of my everyday repertoire.

3 tablespoons Vietnamese fish sauce, preferably Red Boat brand (see Note)

3 tablespoons freshly squeezed lime juice (see note, page 60)

2 tablespoons sugar

1 plump, moist garlic clove, peeled, halved, green germ removed, and minced

1 fresh or dried red bird's eye chile, minced

3 cups (750 ml) watercress leaves

1 thin scallion, white and green parts peeled and sliced into thin rings

A handful of fresh mint leaves, chopped if large

1/3 cup (45 g) roasted and salted peanuts

1. In a small bowl, combine the fish sauce, lime juice, sugar, and 2 tablespoons of water. Stir well to dissolve the sugar. Stir in the garlic and chile.

2. Place the watercress in a salad bowl, pour the dressing over it, and toss well. Add the scallion and mint, and toss once again. Sprinkle with the peanuts and serve.

NOTE: Red Boat fish sauce can be found in Patricia's Pantry at my Amazon Store, accessed via the home page of www.PatriciaWells.com.

MINI PALAIS'S *BURRATA* AND HAM SALAD

~ 4 servings ~

Mini Palais is a large and lovely restaurant in Paris's Grand Palais museum. In good weather, a great way to feel totally Parisian is to settle in on the elegantly casual terrace of this restaurant, where chef consultant Eric Frechon, of the Michelin three-star restaurant Epicure au Bristol, works his modern magic. We enjoyed this appetizer on my first visit early one summer. Use the best cheese you can find, and top-quality, freshly sliced ham. Here I serve it as a large antipasti plate, to be shared.

About 8 ounces (250 g) Italian buffalo-milk *Burrata* or Mozzarella cheese

Extra-virgin olive oil spray

Coarse, freshly ground black pepper

4 ultra-thin slices best-quality Italian San Daniele ham or prosciutto di Parma

2 tablespoons pine nuts, toasted (see Note)

2 sun-dried tomatoes, chopped

16 fresh basil leaves, torn

Arrange the cheese on a large dinner plate. Spray lightly with the oil and season very generously with the pepper. Drape the ham around the edge of the cheese. Scatter with the pine nuts and the sun-dried tomatoes. Spray lightly with oil. Scatter the basil leaves over the top and serve.

NOTE: Toasting pine nuts can be a tricky matter, for they can burn so easily and almost always develop spotty, uneven color. While I generally toast most nuts in a small skillet, watching them carefully, I find that baking pine nuts in the oven results in better, more even toasting. Preheat the oven to 375°F (190°C). Spread the nuts on a baking sheet and bake, stirring occasionally, until an even golden brown, 5 to 10 minutes.

BETSY'S COLD VIETNAMESE SHRIMP AND NOODLE SALAD

~ 4 servings ~

Bun nem nuong is a cold Vietnamese noodle salad that is usually eaten for breakfast. The dish is typically made with small grilled pork meatballs, because pork is one of the meats frequently used in Vietnam. I use shrimp to make it a little healthier. The herbs and lime give it a very fresh flavor on a hot summer day. My good friend Betsy Fox, who first introduced me to Vietnam, kindly shared this recipe.

EQUIPMENT: A steamer.

Noodles

   2 ounces (60 g) thin mung bean vermicelli noodles

Shrimp

   1 pound (500 g) large raw shrimp in the shell, peeled and deveined

   1 tablespoon untoasted sesame oil, such as Leblanc brand

Dressing

   1 fresh or dried red bird's eye chile, sliced into thin rings

   1 cup (125 ml) freshly squeezed lime juice (5 to 9 limes)

   5 tablespoons Vietnamese fish sauce, preferably Red Boat brand (see Note)

   1/3 cup (65 g) sugar

   1 tablespoon minced garlic

Salad

   1 small green papaya (about 1 pound; 500 g), peeled, halved lengthwise, and julienned

   1 European cucumber (about 1 pound; 500g), peeled, halved lengthwise, seeded, and julienned

   6 tablespoons coarsely chopped fresh cilantro

6 tablespoons chiffonade of fresh basil leaves

6 tablespoons coarsely chopped fresh mint leaves

6 tablespoons finely chopped scallions

6 tablespoons coarsely chopped dry-roasted peanuts

1. In a large stockpot, bring 2 quarts (2 l) of water to a boil over high heat. Add the noodles and swirl in the hot water. Cook for 1 minute, or until just tender. Drain thoroughly in a colander and rinse under cold water to prevent the noodles from sticking together. Transfer the noodles to a large bowl and chill.

2. Bring 1 quart (1 l) of water to a simmer in the bottom of a steamer. Arrange the shrimp on the steaming rack. Place the rack over the simmering water, cover, and steam just until the shrimp are pink and cooked through, about 2 minutes. While still warm, toss with the sesame oil.

3. Prepare the dressing: In a medium bowl, soak the red chile in the lime juice for 2 to 3 minutes. Add the remaining dressing ingredients and stir to dissolve the sugar.

4. Pour the dressing over the noodles, add the green papaya, cucumber, herbs, and scallions, and toss. Add the shrimp and top with the chopped peanuts. Serve at room temperature.

NOTE: Red Boat fish sauce can be found in Patricia's Pantry at my Amazon Store, accessed via the home page of www.PatriciaWells.com.

MAKE-AHEAD NOTE: The entire salad can be prepared up to 8 hours in advance and refrigerated. Toss again at serving time.

JUICING A LIME: Now, all of you may already know this, but I didn't until I went to Vietnam. Before that, I juiced limes as I juice lemons, slicing them in half at the equator and extracting the juice with a citrus juicer. Always with great disappointment over the measly quantity of juice, if any! Chef Duc Tran of Mango Mango restaurant in Hoi An, Vietnam, taught me the local method:

Stand the lime on a cutting board, "belly-button" side up. Cutting vertically around the fruit, slice off three generous sections, leaving the fruit in the center as a small triangular wedge. With your hands, squeeze the trio of sections, and be amazed at the quantity of juice extracted! The juice will also be less bitter than the liquid extracted with a citrus juicer.

CHAR-GRILLED EGGPLANT SALAD WITH FRESH MINT

~ 4 servings ~

This Asian-inspired salad is great on a hot day, especially when fresh eggplants are begging to be picked from the garden!

EQUIPMENT: A two-pronged meat fork; a sharp knife or a serrated grapefruit spoon.

‹‹

3 slender purple Asian eggplants (about 1 1/2 pounds; 750 g total)

3 tablespoons Vietnamese fish sauce, preferably Red Boat brand (see Note)

3 tablespoons freshly squeezed lime juice (see note on page 60)

2 tablespoons sugar

1 plump, moist garlic clove, peeled, halved, green germ removed, and minced

1 fresh or dried red bird's eye chile, minced

2 scallions, white and green parts peeled and sliced into thin rings

4 tablespoons coarsely chopped fresh mint leaves

‹‹

1. With the two-pronged meat fork, prick the eggplants all over. Place them directly over an open gas flame, over hot coals, or over an outdoor grill. Cook for 8 to 12 minutes, using tongs to constantly turn the eggplants until the entire skin is darkened, blistered, and has collapsed in on itself. Remove the eggplants from the heat and let cool for 10 minutes.

2. Gently peel the skin away from the flesh with a small, sharp knife or a serrated grapefruit spoon. Be careful to remove all the skin from the flesh and try to keep the eggplant in long strips. (Use paper towels to wipe away any recalcitrant bits of skin.) Arrange the eggplant strips on a platter.

3. In a small bowl, combine the fish sauce, lime juice, 2 tablespoons water, and the sugar. Stir well to dissolve the sugar. Stir in the garlic and chile. Pour the dressing over the eggplant.

4. Scatter the scallions and mint over the dressed eggplant, and serve at room temperature. (The dressed eggplant—without the garnish—can be stored in an airtight container in the refrigerator for up to 1 day. Store the garnish in a separate airtight container. Garnish at serving time.)

NOTE: Red Boat fish sauce can be found in Patricia's Pantry at my Amazon Store, accessed via the home page of www.PatriciaWells.com.

I treasure several plants of pimprenelle, *a hardy perennial known as salad burnet, a "wild" herb that's native to France. I love its cucumber-like flavor and toss it freely into simple green salads or use it as a garnish on soups.*

SOUPS

YELLOW TOMATO SOUP WITH
EVERGREEN TOMATO *TARTARE*
AND RED TOMATO SORBET 66

MUSHROOM-MUSHROOM SOUP
WITH CHORIZO MATCHSTICKS 70

YVELINE'S CHILLED CUCUMBER
AND AVOCADO SOUP WITH
AVOCADO SORBET 73

JERUSALEM ARTICHOKE SOUP
WITH TOASTED PISTACHIOS
AND PISTACHIO OIL 76

SPICY THAI PUMPKIN SOUP
WITH CRAB AND CILANTRO 78

ZUCCHINI AND FRESH
BASIL VELOUTÉ 80

CABBAGE, HAM, POTATO,
AND PEA SOUP 82

TOFU SOUP WITH BOK CHOY,
MINT, AND SCALLIONS 84

WINTER *PISTOU*: PROVENÇAL
VEGETABLE SOUP 85

YELLOW TOMATO SOUP WITH EVERGREEN TOMATO *TARTARE* AND RED TOMATO SORBET

~ 6 servings ~

With the golden Ananas variety of heirloom tomatoes from the garden and a fresh batch of homemade curry powder, this soup comes together in seconds. Be sure to use a very mild olive oil here, because a forward, fruity oil can be overpowering. This soup can stand on its own, or for a bit of glamour it can share the stage with Evergreen Tomato *Tartare* and Red Tomato Sorbet, a trio that I first savored on the terrace of the Paris restaurant Mini Palais.

EQUIPMENT: A blender or a food processor; a 2-inch (5 cm) round pastry cutter, at least 1 1/2 inches (3 cm) high (or use an empty tomato paste can, with both ends removed, as a mold); 6 chilled, shallow soup bowls.

Soup

1 1/2 pounds (750 g) yellow Ananas heirloom tomatoes, cored and quartered (see Note)

1/3 cup (80 ml) mild extra-virgin olive oil

1 teaspoon Homemade Curry Powder (page 282)

1 teaspoon fine sea salt

Evergreen Tomato *Tartare* (recipe follows)

Red Tomato Sorbet (recipe follows)

Small fresh basil leaves, for garnish

1. Combine all the soup ingredients in the blender or food processor. Add 1/3 cup (80 ml) of water. Blend for a full 3 minutes, to create a thick emulsion. Chill until very cold before serving. (Store the soup, covered and refrigerated, for up to 1 day.)

2. When you are ready to serve, place the pastry cutter or mold in the center of a shallow soup bowl. Using a small spoon, spoon the tomato *tartare* into the mold. Carefully remove the mold. Repeat for the remaining soup bowls. Top each serving with a small scoop of the tomato sorbet. Pour the soup around the *tartare*. Garnish the sorbet with a basil leaf, and serve immediately.

NOTE: While I grow many varieties of red, yellow, and green heirloom tomatoes in my garden, a favorite is the yellow Ananas (Pineapple), a tomato that is a pale yellow beefsteak with a red blush on the blossom end and subtle red streaking within the tomato. It is sweet, mildly acidic, and delicious. Other yellow varieties one might find at the farmer's market or grow in the garden include Amber, Aunt Gertie's Gold, Amana Orange, Anna Banana Russian, Oaxacan Jewel, and Valencia. If all else fails, use top-quality red or green tomatoes for the soup.

EVERGREEN TOMATO *TARTARE*

〜 6 servings 〜

While this flavorful tomato *tartare* is part of the trilogy, it also makes a delicious vegetable side dish.

EQUIPMENT: A fine-mesh sieve.

◇◇

2 pounds (1 kg) firm, garden-fresh green heirloom tomatoes, such as Evergreen or Green Zebra

2 shallots, peeled and finely minced

1 teaspoon fresh lemon thyme or regular thyme leaves

2 plump, moist garlic cloves, peeled, halved, green germ removed, finely minced

Fine sea salt

◇◇◇◇◇◇◇◇◇◇◇◇◇◇◇◇◇◇◇◇◇◇◇◇◇◇◇◇◇◇◇◇◇◇◇◇◇◇

Remove the top and bottom of an empty tomato paste can and you have an instant mold for this tomato tartare *and many other goodies.*

1. Core, and with a vegetable peeler, peel the tomatoes. Halve them crosswise (at the equator). Squeeze the tomato halves to release the excess juices and seeds. (The juice and seeds can be reserved to add to soups or sauces.) Cut the tomatoes into 1/8-inch (2.5 mm) cubes and transfer them to the sieve set over a bowl to drain 30 minutes. (This can be done up to 2 hours in advance. Reserve the tomatoes at room temperature.)

2. At serving time, toss the tomatoes with the shallots, lemon thyme, and garlic. Season lightly with salt.

THE SECRET: The tomatoes must be thoroughly drained of their juices so they will hold their shape once molded. Be sure to begin with nice firm tomatoes, not mushy or overripe ones.

RED TOMATO SORBET

I like to serve this refreshing brilliant red sorbet as part of this tomato trio, but it can also serve as a first course palate teaser, garnished with a few basil leaves.

EQUIPMENT: A blender or a food processor; an ice cream maker.

---

2 pounds (1 kg) garden-fresh red heirloom tomatoes, cored and quartered

3/4 cup (185 ml) tomato juice, preferably organic and sodium free

1/2 teaspoon extra-virgin olive oil

1 tablespoon freshly squeezed lime or lemon juice

1 teaspoon Tabasco sauce

1/4 teaspoon fine sea salt

1/4 teaspoon ground *Espelette* pepper, or other mild chile pepper

Fresh basil leaves, for garnish

---

1. In the blender or food processor, combine the tomatoes, tomato juice, oil, lime juice, Tabasco, salt, and *Espelette* pepper and blend until completely smooth, 1 to 2 minutes. Taste for seasoning. Transfer to an airtight container and refrigerate until thoroughly chilled.

2. Close to serving time, transfer the mixture to an ice cream maker and freeze it according to the manufacturer's instructions. Since this makes more sorbet than needed, freeze the extra in scoops on a tray in the freezer and try to consume the same day.

MUSHROOM-MUSHROOM SOUP WITH CHORIZO MATCHSTICKS

～ 8 servings ～

The last time I presented Walter with a bowl of this fragrant, wintry soup, he pronounced it "The Best Ever." Actually, we use that phrase a lot in our house, since, truly, we try to best everything we do here. I must confess that this soup came out as an accident: I had mislabeled some chicken stock in the freezer (not me, the label queen!) and the container actually held morel mushroom liquid. Lucky me that I was going to put it into this mushroom soup because the morel liquid was a revelation. It's mushroom-mushroom soup with dense flavors of the soil. Now of course you can make this with all chicken stock and it will be delicious, but maybe just not The Best Ever! I am always amazed and delighted at what intense pleasure simple button mushrooms can deliver. Cutting the chorizo sausage (I don't cook it) into matchsticks and showering it in the soup adds a nice bit of fatty crunch in the mouth, as well as a welcome smokiness.

EQUIPMENT: A blender or a food processor; 8 warmed, shallow soup bowls.

2 tablespoons (1 ounce; 30 g) unsalted butter

1 leek, white and tender green parts trimmed, rinsed, and minced

1 pound (500 g) button mushrooms, cleaned, stems trimmed, quartered

1 quart (1 l) morel cooking liquid (see page 185) or Homemade Vegetable Stock (page 285)

1 quart (1 l) Homemade Chicken Stock (page 283)

Sea salt

Coarse, freshly ground black pepper

16 thin slices fresh chorizo sausage, cut into matchsticks

1. In a heavy-bottomed stockpot, combine the butter and leek, and sweat—cook, covered, over low heat—until soft, about 5 minutes. Add the mushrooms, morel liquid or vegetable stock, and chicken stock, and season lightly with salt. Cover and simmer for 30 minutes, stirring from time to time.

2. Transfer the soup to the blender or food processor and blend to a smooth liquid. Taste for seasoning. (The soup can be prepared up to 3 days in advance and stored in an airtight container in the refrigerator, or it can be frozen for up to 3 months.)

3. To serve, pour the soup into the warmed soup bowls, season with black pepper, and garnish with the chorizo matchsticks.

YVELINE'S CHILLED CUCUMBER AND AVOCADO SOUP WITH AVOCADO SORBET

~ 8 servings ~

Yveline is our good friend and neighbor in Provence, and she is always coming up with simple local recipes that we love. This is one of her summertime creations. We sometimes add a dollop of avocado sorbet, a fine act of gilding the lily.

EQUIPMENT: A blender or a food processor.

1 large European cucumber (about 1 pound; 500 g), chopped (do not peel)

2 large ripe avocados, halved, pitted, peeled, and cubed

2 cups (500 ml) Homemade Chicken Stock (page 283)

1 cup (45 g) chopped cilantro leaves

1 teaspoon fine sea salt

Grated zest and juice of 1 lime, preferably organic

Avocado Sorbet (recipe follows; optional)

1. In the blender or food processor, combine the cucumber, half of the cubed avocado, the chicken stock, 3/4 cup (34 g) of the cilantro and the salt, and process to blend. Taste for seasoning. Chill for at least 1 hour and up to 24 hours.

2. At serving time, garnish with the remaining 1/4 cup (11 g) cilantro, the rest of the avocado, and the lime juice and zest. If you like, add a spoonful of the sorbet to each bowl.

AVOCADO SORBET

~ 8 servings ~

EQUIPMENT: A blender or a food processor; an ice cream maker.

◇◇◇

2 large ripe avocados, halved, pitted, and peeled

2 cups (500 ml) Greek-style plain whole-milk yogurt

2 teaspoons freshly squeezed lime or lemon juice

1/4 teaspoon ground *Espelette* pepper or other mild chile pepper

1/4 teaspoon fine sea salt

1 teaspoon honey

2 tablespoons Invert Sugar Syrup (page 75) or light corn syrup

◇◇◇

1. Combine all the ingredients in the blender or food processor. Blend until completely smooth, 1 to 2 minutes. Taste for seasoning. Chill completely.

2. At serving time, transfer the chilled mixture to an ice cream maker and freeze according to the manufacturer's instructions. For best results, serve the sorbet as soon as it is frozen. Do not re-freeze.

INVERT SUGAR SYRUP

~ Makes about 1 3/4 cups (435 ml) ~

Invert sugar is basically a very thick, clear sugar syrup, with the consistency of liquid honey or light corn syrup. The French call it *tremoline.* The syrup makes for a smoother mouth feel in sorbets and ice creams and also controls crystallization. It is simple to make, and stores for up to 6 months in the refrigerator.

EQUIPMENT: A 2-quart (2 l) stainless steel sauce pan.

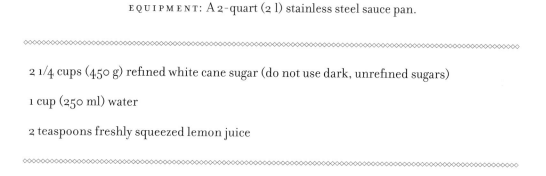

2 1/4 cups (450 g) refined white cane sugar (do not use dark, unrefined sugars)

1 cup (250 ml) water

2 teaspoons freshly squeezed lemon juice

In the saucepan, combine the ingredients and bring to a boil over high heat. Do not stir. Reduce the heat to low and simmer until the mixture is slightly thick and viscous, like corn syrup or a liquid honey, 10 to 12 minutes. The mixture should not darken or caramelize. Be aware that the liquid will thicken as it cools. I find it better to err on the runny side, rather than risking a syrup that is too thick and nearly impossible to pour. Transfer to a heatproof jar and let cool. Cover and refrigerate for up to 6 months.

JERUSALEM ARTICHOKE SOUP WITH TOASTED PISTACHIOS AND PISTACHIO OIL

~ 8 servings ~

How can this gnarled and knobby vegetable offer such elegance? This soup deserves a pedestal, as the creamy alabaster liquid mingles with the equally regal pistachio oil and brilliant green toasted pistachios. The soup elicits looks of surprise from guests, followed by sounds of happy pleasure.

EQUIPMENT: A blender or a food processor; 8 warmed, shallow soup bowls.

2 quarts (2 l) whole milk

2 teaspoons fine sea salt

2 pounds (1 kg) Jerusalem artichokes (sunchokes), scrubbed

1/4 cup (30 g) salted pistachios, toasted, for garnish

Best-quality pistachio oil, such as Leblanc brand, for garnish

1. Rinse a large saucepan with water, leaving a bit of water in the pan (this will prevent the milk from scorching and sticking to the pan). Pour the milk into the pan and add the salt.

2. Trim and peel the Jerusalem artichokes, and chop them coarsely, dropping them into the milk as you work (this will stop the vegetable from turning brown as it is exposed to the air). When all the Jerusalem artichokes are prepared, place the pan over medium heat and cook gently until they are soft, 35 to 40 minutes. Watch carefully so the milk does not boil over. The milk may curdle, but that will not alter the texture or flavor of the final soup.

3. Transfer the mixture, in small batches, to the blender or food processor. Do not place the plunger in the feed tube of the food processor or in the lid of the blender, or the heat will create a vacuum and the liquid will splatter. Puree until the mixture is perfectly smooth and silken, 1 to 2 minutes.

4. Return the soup to the saucepan and reheat gently. Taste for seasoning. Transfer it to the warmed, shallow soup bowls, shower with the pistachios, and drizzle with pistachio oil.

SPICY THAI PUMPKIN SOUP WITH CRAB AND CILANTRO

~ 8 servings ~

The preparation for a weeklong "off site" cooking class in Vietnam brought me to this recipe, which has become a school and family favorite, with the fragrance and flavors of curry paste, ginger, coconut, and citrus.

EQUIPMENT: A blender or a food processor; 8 warmed, shallow soup bowls.

3 shallots, peeled and finely minced

2 tablespoons Thai yellow curry paste, preferably organic

3 tablespoons grated fresh ginger

1 pound (500 g) pumpkin or butternut squash, cubed (or 2 cups; 500 ml canned pumpkin puree)

One 28-ounce (765 g) can peeled Italian plum tomatoes in juice

3 cups (750 ml) Homemade Vegetable Stock (page 285) or Homemade Chicken Stock (page 283)

1 cup (250 ml) coconut juice, preferably organic

2 tablespoons freshly squeezed lime or lemon juice

1 tablespoon Vietnamese fish sauce, preferably Red Boat brand (see Note)

7 ounces (200 g) fresh crabmeat

Fresh cilantro leaves, for garnish

1. In a large saucepan, combine the shallots, curry paste, and ginger and cook over low heat until the shallots are soft and the mixture is well combined, 2 to 3 minutes. Set aside 1 tablespoon of the mixture for garnish.

2. Add the pumpkin, tomatoes (with juices), and vegetable or chicken stock and simmer, covered, for 15 minutes or until the pumpkin is tender. Transfer to the blender or food processor and puree.

3. Return the mixture to the saucepan and add the coconut juice. Stir to blend. Bring back to a simmer. Stir in the lime juice and fish sauce.

4. Place several tablespoons of the crabmeat in the center of each soup bowl. Pour the soup all around the crabmeat. Garnish with the reserved curry-ginger mixture and a sprinkle of cilantro leaves.

MAKE-AHEAD NOTE: Complete the recipe through step 2. Store in an airtight container in the refrigerator for up to 3 days. Complete at serving time.

NOTE: Red Boat fish sauce can be found in Patricia's Pantry at my Amazon Store, accessed via the home page of www.PatriciaWells.com.

ZUCCHINI AND FRESH BASIL VELOUTÉ

~ 8 servings ~

My good friend Brian Huggler has a thriving garden in Lansing, Michigan, and is an enthusiastic and creative cook. He prepared this appealing soup one evening in early September in Provence. Before I had a second spoonful of this versatile starter, I begged for the recipe. He sent it right away, noting that it had that special Lansing touch: this soup can be served cold or hot, summer or winter. I like to stash a small batch in my freezer for the cold winter months, when the soup brings the sunshine of summer into my life on a gloomy day. Smooth and a brilliant green with flecks of dark green, the soup is beautiful in its simplicity, and the peppery hit of basil comes through loud and clear.

EQUIPMENT: A blender or a food processor; 8 warmed, or chilled, shallow soup bowls.

2 tablespoons extra-virgin olive oil

2 medium onions, peeled, halved lengthwise, and cut into very thin half-moons

Fine sea salt

2 pounds (1 kg) firm zucchini, rinsed, trimmed, and cut into small pieces (do not peel)

1 quart (1 l) Homemade Chicken Stock (page 283) or Homemade Vegetable Stock (page 285)

1 bunch fresh basil leaves (about 1/2 cup; 5 g firmly packed)

1. In a stockpot, combine the oil, onions, and salt, and sweat—cook, covered, over low heat until soft and translucent—3 to 5 minutes. Add the zucchini and stock and bring to a simmer. Simmer, covered, until the zucchini is cooked through, about 15 minutes.

2. Remove from the heat. In the blender or food processor, combine the zucchini mixture with the basil leaves and puree to a smooth liquid. Taste for seasoning. Serve hot or chilled, in warmed or chilled soup bowls. (Store in an airtight container in the refrigerator for up to 3 days. Or freeze in airtight containers for up to 3 months. Reblend at serving time.)

When students present me with one of their preparations, the first thing I ask is, "How does it taste?" Quite often they haven't tasted, just followed the recipe. "Taste, taste, taste" is one of my commandments. There are always an ample number of tasting spoons in each cooking area.

CABBAGE, HAM, POTATO, AND PEA SOUP

~ 6 servings ~

In the cold months, this hearty soup warms the house as well as the soul.

EQUIPMENT: 6 warmed, shallow soup bowls.

5 ounces (150 g) smoked bacon, rind removed, cut into 1/4-inch (5 mm) cubes (1 1/2 cups; 375 ml)

10 ounces (300 g) firm, yellow-fleshed potatoes, such as Yukon Gold (do not peel), cubed

3 celery ribs, thinly sliced

1 medium onion, peeled and thinly sliced

1 medium leek, white and tender green parts only, trimmed, rinsed, and thinly sliced

5 plump, moist garlic cloves, peeled, halved, and green germ removed

2 quarts (2 l) Homemade Chicken Stock (page 283), heated

10 ounces (300 g) Savoy cabbage (about 1/4 head), thinly sliced

10 ounces (300 g) frozen peas (no need to thaw)

Fine sea salt

Coarse, freshly ground black pepper

Toasted sourdough bread, for serving

1. In large stockpot, brown the bacon over moderate heat until crisp and golden, about 5 minutes. With a slotted spoon, transfer the bacon to paper towels to absorb the fat. Blot the top of the bacon with paper towels as well.

2. Return the bacon to the stockpot. Add the potatoes, celery, onion, leek, and garlic, and sweat—cook, covered, over low heat—until the potatoes start to soften, 4 to 5 minutes. Add the hot stock and simmer until the potatoes are tender, about 15 minutes more. Add the cabbage and peas and simmer for just 1 to 2 minutes, to keep the cabbage and peas a bright green. Season with salt and pepper.

3. Serve hot, with toasted sourdough bread.

TOFU SOUP WITH BOK CHOY, MINT, AND SCALLIONS

~ 4 to 6 servings ~

Our cooking class in Vietnam inspired this fresh, fragrant, healthy, any-season soup, welcome on the table at all times.

~~~~~~

6 cups (1.5 l) Homemade Chicken Stock (page 283) or Homemade Vegetable Stock (page 285)

1 bunch fresh Vietnamese mint (*rau ram*) or regular mint, plus extra leaves for garnish

1 tablespoon coarse sea salt

6 ounces (180 g) baby bok choy, rinsed, root ends trimmed and leaves separated, cut into bite-size pieces (or use spinach)

8 ounces (250 g) fresh cultivated mushrooms, rinsed, trimmed, and sliced

Fine sea salt

Freshly ground black pepper

10 ounces (300 g) medium-firm tofu, rinsed, drained, and cut into 1-inch (2.5 cm) cubes

3 thin scallions, green parts only, trimmed and thinly sliced diagonally

~~~~~~

1. Pour the stock into a stockpot and bring it to a gentle boil over medium heat. Reduce the heat to medium-low, add the mint, and simmer, partially covered, until ready to use.

2. Meanwhile, bring 1 quart (1 l) water to a boil in a saucepan. Add the coarse sea salt and blanch the bok choy leaves until cooked but still firm, about 1 minute. With a slotted spoon, transfer the bok choy to a colander to drain.

3. Add the bok choy and the mushrooms to the stock. Season to taste with fine sea salt and pepper, and simmer for 4 minutes. Remove the bunch of mint. Add the tofu and simmer until it is heated through, about 2 minutes more. Serve hot, garnished with extra mint and the scallions.

WINTER *PISTOU*: PROVENÇAL VEGETABLE SOUP

~ 16 servings ~

Summer *pistou*—the famed Provençal soup made with summer's vegetable bounty and the fresh white shell beans known as *cocos blancs*—is the first recipe we prepare in our Provençal cooking classes in summer and fall. Here is my winter version, using winter's bounty and beans that I shell in the summertime and freeze for winter pleasures. In this variation, I've replaced green beans and zucchini with celery and pumpkin, use canned tomatoes instead of fresh, and *épeautre* (spelt) in place of pasta. I don't serve it with the classic fresh basil and garlic sauce, but rather like it with a good hit of freshly ground black pepper as well as freshly grated Pecorino Romano cheese (instead of Swiss Gruyère) for a more wintry and pungent flavor. As always I use two different cheeses—here Pecorino and Parmesan—for a more sophisticated and complex mix of flavors.

5 tablespoons extra-virgin olive oil

3 plump, moist garlic cloves, peeled and halved lengthwise, green germ removed

4 medium onions, peeled, halved crosswise, and cut into thin half moons

3 medium leeks, white and tender green parts only, rinsed, quartered, and thinly sliced

Bouquet garni: several fresh or dried bay leaves, fresh celery leaves, thyme sprigs, and parsley sprigs, encased in a wire-mesh tea infuser or bound in a piece of cheesecloth

Fine sea salt

8 medium carrots, scrubbed and cut into thin disks

1 pound (500 g) firm, yellow-fleshed potatoes, such as Yukon Gold, peeled and cubed

4 celery ribs with leaves, cut into thin pieces

2 pounds (1 kg) raw pumpkin, peeled and cubed (to yield 1 quart; 1 l)

1 cup *épeautre* (spelt), rinsed and drained

One 28-ounce (750 g) can peeled Italian plum tomatoes in juice

2 tablespoons Italian tomato paste

1 pound (500 g) fresh small white (navy) beans in the pod, shelled; or 8 ounces (250 g) dried small white beans, soaked (see Note)

1 pound (500 g) fresh cranberry beans in the pod, shelled; or 8 ounces (250 g) dried cranberry beans, soaked (see Note)

Coarse, freshly ground black pepper

3/4 cup (50 g) freshly grated Pecorino Romano cheese

3/4 cup (75 g) freshly grated Parmigiano-Reggiano cheese

---

1. In a large, heavy-bottomed stockpot, combine the oil, garlic, onions, leeks, bouquet garni, and salt to taste. Stir to coat with the oil. Sweat—cook, covered, over low heat—until the garlic is fragrant and soft, about 2 minutes. Add the carrots, potatoes, celery, pumpkin, *épeautre*, tomatoes (with juices), tomato paste, and 4 quarts (4 l) of cold water. Cover and bring to a simmer. Simmer for 30 minutes.

2. Add the navy and cranberry beans and cook until tender, about 30 minutes. (Cooking time will vary according to the freshness of the beans. Add more water if the soup becomes too thick.)

3. Increase the heat to high and boil the soup for 5 minutes (this thickens the soup, creating rich flavors and a luxurious texture). Taste for seasoning. Remove and discard the bouquet garni. Serve the soup very hot, seasoned with black pepper and the grated cheeses.

NOTE: If using dried beans: Rinse the beans, picking them over to remove any pebbles. Place the beans in a large bowl, add boiling water to cover, and set aside for 1 hour. Drain the beans, discarding the water. Use as indicated in the recipe.

THE SECRET: Years ago while making a batch of summer *pistou* I looked at the clock and it was time to eat. The soup was not quite finished, so I turned up the heat and boiled it for 5 minutes. It turned out to be the Best Ever version of this soup, so I've followed this principle ever since!

While traditionally one will wrap herbs and spices in cheesecloth tied with cotton twine, I find that a stainless steel wire mesh tea infuser is quicker and more practical for infusing.

I am the label queen. Take a look in my freezer and you'll find everything neatly labeled and dated—a simple habit that makes life so much easier! In the kitchen, I also label all spices, salts, and so on, so there is no question as to what is in the jar.

PROVENCE

An old well house and an old oaken bucket for bringing up water.

Food comes to the table for a luncheon feast in Provence.

Grenache, Syrah, and Mourvèdre grapes make up the bulk of the grape varieties in our vineyard—all good, all local, all delicious for a lovely Clos Chanteduc Côtes-du-Rhône.

FISH & SHELLFISH

MUSSELS WITH LEMON, CAPERS,
JALAPEÑO, AND CILANTRO 92

SALMON SASHIMI WITH
AN AVALANCHE OF HERBS 94

OYSTERS SEARED WITH
PANCETTA AND *SHISO* 97

GOLDEN ALMOND-CRUSTED
SOLE FILLETS 99

STEAMED *YUZU* SCALLOPS ON
A BED OF SESAME SEA GREENS 101

SHRIMP IN SPICY
COCONUT BROTH 103

STEAMED SHRIMP WITH
SESAME OIL, BLACK RICE,
PEAS, AND SCALLIONS 105

MUSSELS WITH LEMON, CAPERS, JALAPEÑO, AND CILANTRO

~ 4 servings ~

Mussels are healthy, inexpensive, and sustainable. The fact that their rich, meaty, sea-fresh flavor is delicious means that they find their way to our table with great frequency. Here they are embellished simply with a vinaigrette heightened by the tang of capers, jalapeño peppers, and cilantro. A quick, easy, protein-rich meal at its best.

EQUIPMENT: A large deep skillet with a lid.

2 pounds (1 kg) fresh mussels

1/4 cup (60 ml) extra-virgin olive oil

1 tablespoon freshly squeezed lemon juice

Grated zest of 1 lemon, preferably organic

1/4 cup (60 ml) capers in vinegar, drained

2 shallots, peeled and finely minced

2 tablespoons chopped pickled jalapeño peppers

2 scallions, white and green parts, trimmed and peeled and cut into thin rings

6 tablespoons minced fresh cilantro leaves

Coarse, freshly ground black pepper

Crusty bread, for serving

1. Thoroughly scrub the mussels, and rinse them with several changes of water. If an open mussel closes when you press on it, then it is good; if it stays open, the mussel should be discarded.

Beard the mussels: With your fingers, pull off and discard the string-like beard that hangs from the shellfish. (Do not beard the mussels more than a few minutes in advance or they will die and spoil. Note that in some markets mussels are pre-prepared, in that the small black beard has been clipped off but not entirely removed. These mussels do not need further attention.)

2. In a large salad bowl, combine the oil, lemon juice, lemon zest, capers, shallots, and jalapeño peppers. Whisk to blend.

3. Place the mussels in a skillet that is large enough to hold them once the mussels have opened. Cover, and steam the mussels open over high heat, just 2 to 3 minutes. Do not overcook. Discard any mussels that do not open.

4. While the mussels are still hot, pour the opened mussels and their liquid into the salad bowl. Toss to coat the mussels with the vinaigrette. Garnish with the scallions and cilantro, and season generously with pepper. Serve immediately, with plenty of crusty bread to soak up the sauce.

THE SECRET: Toss the mussels with the dressing while they are still warm so the shellfish better absorb the flavors.

WINE SUGGESTION: I like a pure, crisp white here. Try Domaine Trimbach's easy Riesling: light and refreshing and a fine match for this zesty mussel dish.

SALMON SASHIMI WITH AN AVALANCHE OF HERBS

~ 6 servings ~

This is one of the more versatile fish dishes I can imagine. Inspired by Vietnamese cooking, it is the sort of recipe that can link itself to almost any cuisine. All you need is an avalanche of herbs (preferably four or five for variety and pungency) and a sauce that packs a wallop (Vietnamese dipping sauce is ideal here). And though my first instinct is to make this with salmon, the possibilities are endless. Any ultra-fresh fish could be used here, including scallops, halibut, or any other firm whitefish fillets. I can go wild with herbs: the last time I made this, I created a mix of tarragon, basil, mint, chives, and *shiso* as well as strips of dried seaweed, or *nori.* I would stay away from fresh herbs that can be overly pungent, such as sage or oregano.

1 pound (500 g) ultra-fresh, sashimi-grade salmon

1 packed cup (15 g) mixed fresh herbs, such as basil, mint, *shiso,* and cilantro, rinsed and patted dry

1 to 2 tablespoons Vietnamese Dipping Sauce (page 293), plus extra for serving

Lime wedges, for serving

1. Slice the salmon as thin as possible and arrange the slices on individual salad plates.

2. Finely mince the herbs and scatter them evenly over the salmon.

3. At serving time, sprinkle with the dipping sauce. Serve with the lime wedges and additional sauce alongside.

WINE SUGGESTION: A floral white is ideal here. We often enjoy the sashimi with Olivier Leflaive's 100% Chardonnay Bourgogne blanc, always a good-value white Burgundy.

THE SECRET: An avalanche of fresh herbs. You can never have too many or too many varieties.

VARIATION: Marinate the salmon in the dipping sauce and sprinkle with thinly sliced lemongrass for added punch and Asian flavor.

OYSTERS SEARED WITH PANCETTA AND *SHISO*

～ 6 servings as an appetizer, 2 servings as a main course ～

Students enjoy preparing these salty oyster "packets" with the hidden surprise of *shiso* leaf inside: the Asian leaves, also known as *perilla,* are a great boon to cooks who love their intense herbal flavors, almost a mix of strong mint and fennel with a heady fragrance. For best results, prepare these packets at the very last moment.

EQUIPMENT: Toothpicks.

12 large, fresh oysters in the shell

12 ultra-thin pancetta slices

12 large *shiso* leaves, or 12 large basil leaves or 12 small spinach leaves

2 teaspoons extra-virgin olive oil

Lemon wedges, for serving

1. Open the oysters, and cut the muscle to extract them from the shell. Place the oysters in a bowl.

2. Place the bottoms of the oyster shells in a bowl of hot water to keep them warm.

3. Place a slice of pancetta on a clean work surface. Place a *shiso* leaf on top. Place an oyster on top of the *shiso* leaf. Fold the pancetta packet lengthwise in half, securing the packet with a toothpick. Repeat for the remaining oysters.

4. Remove the oyster shells from the hot water and arrange them either on oyster plates or on a bed of coarse salt.

5. In a large skillet, heat the oil over moderate heat until it is hot but not smoking. Reduce the heat to low. Carefully arrange the oyster packets side by side in the skillet. Cook until the pancetta browns, about 30 seconds. Turn the packets over and cook for about 30 seconds more.

6. Remove and discard the toothpicks. Transfer the oyster packets to the prepared oyster shells. Serve as an appetizer or as a main course, passing lemon wedges for seasoning.

WINE SUGGESTION: With oysters, a longtime natural white comes from the seaside vineyards of Muscadet: try the soft and light Muscadet de Sèvre et Maine sur Lie from winemaker André-Michel Brégeon.

Each spring I plant both red and green shiso—the pungent Japanese herb embellishing sushi and sashimi—and I love to pair it with just about every kind of fish and shellfish. It's great when wrapped around oysters, then enveloped in thin slices of pancetta and seared.

GOLDEN ALMOND-CRUSTED SOLE FILLETS

~ 4 servings ~

I first sampled this fish one sunny day in June, on the magical terrace of Mini Palais, the restaurant situated inside the Grand Palais museum in Paris. This is such an easy, quick, delicious dish and one that we often make in class. The entire dish can be prepared several hours in advance, and one can easily adjust the number, baking enough fillets to serve two or twenty!

EQUIPMENT: A nonstick baking sheet lined with baking parchment.

4 tablespoons (60 g) unsalted butter

4 tablespoons (30 g) almond meal (see Notes)

Fine sea salt

Coarse, freshly ground black pepper

8 fresh white-fleshed fish fillets, about 3 ounces (90 g) each (see Notes)

1/2 cup (40 g) sliced almonds

1. In a small pan, melt the butter. Remove from the heat and stir in the almond meal. Season with salt and pepper and stir again. Leave aside to cool to room temperature and harden enough to spread, about 1 hour. (Do not refrigerate. The mixture may become too firm to spread.)

2. Center a rack in the oven. Preheat the oven to 400°F (200°C).

3. Place the fillets side by side on the baking sheet. Season with salt and pepper.

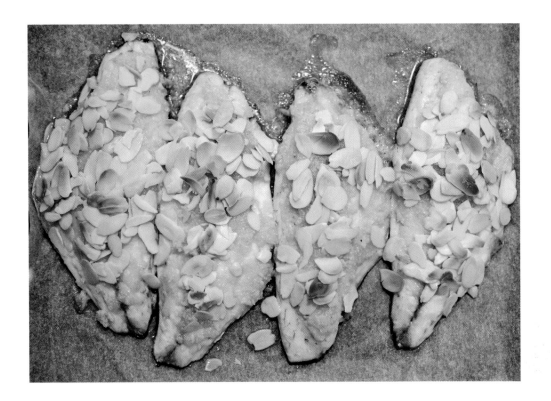

4. Spread the cooled almond butter paste over the fillets. Cover the paste with a layer of sliced almonds. Place in the oven and bake the fillets for 4 minutes. To test for doneness, pierce a fillet with a knife set at a 45-degree angle. The fish should be opaque and should flake. If the almonds are not sufficiently colored, place the fillets under the broiler until golden. Serve immediately.

WINE SUGGESTION: On that golden day we sampled the golden white from winemaker Olivier Merlin. His Macon la Roche Vineuse is pure, mineral-rich, a pleasure, and a fine match for this almond-flecked fish dish.

NOTES:

• Almond meal (sometimes called almond flour or ground almonds) is made from whole, unblanched (skin-on) almonds. For this recipe, whole, unblanched almonds can be finely ground in a food processor. Do not over-process or you may end up with almond butter.

• Any firm, white-fleshed fish fillets can be used here, such as halibut, flounder, trout, or perch.

STEAMED *YUZU* SCALLOPS ON A BED OF SESAME SEA GREENS

~ 4 servings ~

From October to May, we get the most plump, delicious scallops. I love to give them an Asian flavor, pairing them with the juice of the fragrant Japanese citrus *yuzu* and steaming them on a bed of sea greens.

EQUIPMENT: A wok or a large skillet; a bamboo steamer; 4 warmed salad plates.

---

12 large or 16 medium scallops (roe detached, if present)

2 tablespoons plus 2 teaspoons best-quality toasted sesame oil, such as Leblanc brand

2 teaspoons *yuzu* juice or freshly squeezed lemon or lime juice

Fleur de sel

1 package sea greens (wakame), rinsed, sliced like linguine

---

1. Slice each scallop crosswise on the diagonal into 3 even pieces.

2. In a bowl, combine the 2 tablespoons sesame oil and the citrus juice. Add the scallops, toss gently to coat, and season with *fleur de sel*. Marinate for 20 minutes.

3. Meanwhile, in a medium bowl, toss the sea greens with the 2 teaspoons sesame oil.

4. Bring 1 quart (1 l) of water to a simmer in the wok. Arrange the sea greens on the bamboo steamer rack. Arrange the scallops and the roe, if present, on top of the greens. Cover the steamer, place it in the wok over simmering water, and steam for 2 minutes for rare scallops, or cook to your desired doneness.

5. Transfer the scallops and sea green to the warmed salad plates, and serve.

WINE SUGGESTION: White, white, white with this! Let's stay with a favorite Macon white, the 100% Chardonnay Macon-Villages Quintaine from the Domaine Guillemot-Michel, a biodynamically farmed vineyard with wines full of lovely honey and fruit flavors—apple, lemon—a wine that also loves the scent of the sea.

SHRIMP IN SPICY COCONUT BROTH

~ 4 servings ~

This alluring dish can be put together in a matter of minutes using top-quality, freshly cooked shrimp. Either homemade curry paste or a good brand of imported paste can be used here.

EQUIPMENT: A wok or a large, deep skillet; 4 warmed, shallow soup bowls.

4 ounces (125 g) snow peas, trimmed

2 tablespoons vegetable oil

2 tablespoons Homemade Curry Paste (page 107) or good-quality purchased curry paste

1 1/2 cups (375 ml) light coconut milk, shaken to blend, or coconut water

1/2 cup (125 ml) Homemade Vegetable Stock (page 285)

1 tablespoon brown sugar

4 fresh or dried kaffir lime leaves (optional, see Note)

1 pound (500 g) large cooked shrimp, peeled and deveined

2 tablespoons freshly squeezed lime juice

2 tablespoons Vietnamese fish sauce, preferably Red Boat brand (see Note on page 56)

3 tablespoons fresh cilantro leaves, for garnish

1. Bring a medium pot of water to a boil, and fill a bowl with ice water. Blanch the snow peas in the boiling water for 2 minutes; then drain, and refresh them in the ice water.

2. In the wok or skillet, heat the oil over moderate heat. Add the curry paste and stir for 30 seconds. Add the coconut milk, stock, brown sugar, and kaffir lime leaves, if using. Simmer, uncovered,

for 3 minutes. Add the shrimp and heat through for 1 minute. Add the lime juice and fish sauce and stir to blend. Remove and discard the lime leaves, if using. Taste for seasoning.

3. With a slotted spoon, divide the shrimp and snow peas among the four warmed soup bowls. Pour the broth into each bowl. Garnish with the cilantro leaves, and serve.

WINE SUGGESTION: In our classes students love one of our favorite "daily drinking whites," Domaine Alary's Cairanne Font d'Estévenas blanc, a blend of Clairette and Roussanne and a wine that loves food and spice.

NOTE: Dried kaffir lime leaves and Red Boat fish sauce can be found in Patricia's Pantry at my Amazon Store, accessed via the home page of www.PatriciaWells.com.

STEAMED SHRIMP WITH SESAME OIL, BLACK RICE, PEAS, AND SCALLIONS

～ 4 servings ～

This dish is worth preparing if only to enjoy the nutty, warm fragrance that fills the kitchen as the aromatic black rice cooks away. Likewise, the bright aroma of the steamed shrimp as they soak up the sesame oil. The peas add a brilliant touch of green, and the scallions that essential crunch.

EQUIPMENT: A steamer.

1 cup (150 g) black rice (see Note)

2 teaspoons fine sea salt

1 pound (500 g) large raw shrimp, peeled and deveined

2 teaspoons best-quality sesame oil, such as Leblanc brand

1 cup (125 g) frozen peas, thawed

4 scallions, white and green parts trimmed and cut into thin rings

1. In a large saucepan, combine the rice, salt, and 2 quarts (2 l) of water. Bring to a boil, reduce the heat to a simmer, and cook, uncovered, until the rice is cooked but still firm to the bite, 20 to 30 minutes. (I find the rice is easy to undercook but almost impossible to overcook.) Drain through a fine-mesh sieve, discarding any water in the saucepan.

2.   While the rice cooks, bring 1 quart (1 l) of water to a simmer in the bottom of a steamer. Arrange the shrimp on the steaming rack. Place the rack over the simmering water, cover, and steam just until the shrimp are pink and cooked through, about 2 minutes. In a medium bowl, toss the warm shrimp with the sesame oil.

3.   In a large bowl, combine the drained rice, the peas, and the scallions and toss to blend. Taste for seasoning. To serve, spoon the rice onto the center of each plate. Arrange the shrimp alongside.

WINE SUGGESTION: When preparing this with students in my Paris class, we paired it with the white Irouléguy from the Basque region of France; the Domaine Arretxea is a complex blend of Gros Manseng, Petit Manseng, and Petit Courbu, a high-mountain wine that seems to love the nutty flavors of the black rice.

NOTE: Black rice can be found at Asian markets or in Patricia's Pantry at my Amazon Store, accessed via the home page of www.PatriciaWells.com.

HOMEMADE CURRY PASTE

~ Makes 1/2 cup (125 ml) ~

EQUIPMENT: An electric spice mill; a blender or a food processor.

2 teaspoons coriander seeds

1 teaspoon cumin seeds

1 teaspoon fennel seeds

1 teaspoon black peppercorns, preferably Tellicherry

A small handful fresh cilantro leaves

A 2-inch (5 cm) piece of fresh ginger, peeled and chopped

1 lemongrass stalk (bottom third only), trimmed, outer leaves removed, sliced paper-thin

1 tablespoon finely ground dried red chiles

2 shallots, peeled and chopped

4 plump, moist garlic cloves, peeled, halved, green germ removed

Grated zest of 1 lime, preferably organic

1 1/2 teaspoons fine sea salt

1 teaspoon freshly grated nutmeg

1/3 cup (80 ml) neutral oil, such as grapeseed oil

1. In a small, dry skillet, combine the coriander, cumin, fennel, and peppercorns and toast over moderate heat, shaking the pan to prevent burning, for 2 to 3 minutes. Remove from the heat and let cool. In the spice mill, grind to a fine powder.

2. In the blender or food processor, combine the cilantro, ginger, lemongrass, chile, shallots, garlic, lime zest, salt, and nutmeg and process until finely chopped. Add the toasted spices and, with the machine running, slowly add the oil. Taste for seasoning. Transfer to an airtight container, and refrigerate for up to 1 week.

POULTRY & MEAT

WALTER'S SALT AND PEPPER STEAK 111

SEARED DUCK BREAST WITH FRESH
FIGS AND BLACK CURRANT SAUCE 113

RABBIT WITH MUSTARD
AND TARRAGON 116

BRAISED CABBAGE WITH
SMOKED SAUSAGE AND MUSTARD 119

FRICASSÉE OF CHICKEN
WITH FENNEL, CAPERS,
ARTICHOKES, AND TOMATOES 121

BEEF DAUBE WITH
FRESH PASTA SQUARES 124

LEMON-CURED
SIRLOIN CARPACCIO 129

CHAR-GRILLED PORK PATTIES 130

FOUR-HOUR AROMATIC
STAR ANISE—BRAISED PORK 133

WALTER'S SALT AND PEPPER STEAK

~ 4 servings ~

I am not sure why, but a thick, juicy *côte de boeuf* calls for a party—a simple but festive meal enjoyed with friends around the table, a sturdy red wine, and a simple green salad. This recipe demands no more gadgetry than a well-seasoned skillet. Walter remembers watching his father cook steaks, and he always heated coarse sea salt and waited until it "danced" before cooking the meat. It's an uncomplicated but sure-fire way to ensure a thick, flavorful crust on one of our favorite cuts of meat.

EQUIPMENT: A griddle, seasoned cast-iron skillet, or heavy-duty skillet.

1 bone-in beef rib steak, about 2 pounds (1 kg), about 1 inch (2.5 cm) thick

2 tablespoons coarse sea salt

Coarse, freshly ground black pepper

Fleur de sel

Lemon wedges, for serving

1. Remove the meat from the refrigerator at least 30 minutes before cooking.

2. When you are ready to cook the beef, preheat the griddle or skillet over high heat for 2 minutes. Scatter the coarse sea salt on the griddle and heat until the salt "dances," or begins to pop, about 3 minutes. Then add the meat, unseasoned, and cook for 4 minutes on one side. Turn the meat, season the seared side with pepper, and cook for 4 minutes more for rare meat, or cook to desired doneness.

In cooking—and in particular with grilled meats—seasoning is everything.

3. Transfer the meat to a cutting board. Season the second side with pepper and season both sides with *fleur de sel.* Tent the meat loosely with foil to prevent the surface from cooling off too quickly. Let it rest for 5 to 10 minutes.

4. To serve, carve into thick slices. Serve with lemon wedges.

THE SECRET: Three rules here: sear, season, rest. Searing caramelizes and browns the proteins on the surface of the meat, resulting in more intense flavors and an attractive crust. The salt does help begin to season the meat, but because the pan is extremely hot, the meat begins to sear immediately, forming a crust that prevents the salt from drawing moisture from the steak. The final seasoning makes for meat that tastes seasoned, not salted. Resting allows the juices to retreat back into the meat, resulting in beef that is moist and tender, not dry.

WINE SUGGESTION: Bring out a sturdy red that will stand up to the forward flavors of well-cooked beef. With this meat I like to uncork our winemaker Yves Gras's stellar cuvée, Gigondas Prestige des Hautes Garrigues. The wine is a blend of 80 percent old-vine Grenache, 15 percent Mourvèdre, 3 percent Syrah, and 1 percent Cinsaut. It's aged for 2 years in oak barrels and oak tanks and bottled without filtration. A perfect match for a perfectly cooked steak.

SEARED DUCK BREAST WITH FRESH FIGS AND BLACK CURRANT SAUCE

~ 4 servings ~

This is a "Monday night special" in our cooking class in Provence. Our local butcher supplies the most delicious, meaty duck breasts, and a variety of fresh figs are in season from June to October. This super-easy all-purpose sauce could also be used on any grilled or roasted poultry. I use a good-quality balsamic vinegar here, but nothing super-thick or aged. Two brands that I most respect are Rustichella d'Abruzzo and Leonardi.

EQUIPMENT: A warmed platter; 4 warmed dinner plates.

16 fresh figs

2 fatted duck breasts (*magret*), each about 1 pound (500 g)

Fine sea salt

Coarse, freshly ground black pepper

1/2 cup (125 ml) best-quality balsamic vinegar (see Note)

1 cup (250 ml) *crème de cassis* (black currant liqueur) or black currant juice

1. Stand each fig, stem end up, on a cutting board. Trim off and discard the stem end of the fig. Make an X-shaped incision into each fig, cutting about one-third of the way down through the fruit.

2. Remove the duck from the refrigerator 10 minutes in advance before cooking. With a sharp knife, make about 10 diagonal incisions in the skin of each duck breast. Make about 10 additional diagonal incisions to create a crisscross pattern. The cuts should be deep but should not go all

the way through to the flesh. (The scoring will help the fat melt while cooking and will stop the duck breast from shrinking up as it cooks.) Season the breasts all over with salt and pepper.

3. Heat a dry skillet over medium heat. When the pan is warm, place the breasts, skin side down, in the pan. Reduce the heat to low and cook gently until the skin is a uniform, deep golden brown, about 3 minutes. Carefully remove and discard the fat in the pan. Cook the breasts skin side up for 10 minutes more for medium-rare duck, or cook to desired doneness.

4. Remove the duck from the skillet and place the breasts side by side on the warmed platter. Season generously with salt and pepper. Tent loosely with foil and let the duck rest for at least 10 minutes, to allow the juices to retreat back into the meat.

5. In a small saucepan, combine the vinegar and *crème de cassis* and warm over low heat.

6. In a saucepan that will hold the figs snugly, arrange them tightly in a single layer, cut end up. Pour the warm vinegar mixture over the figs and cook over low heat, basting the figs with the liquid, for about 3 minutes.

7. Cut the duck breasts on the diagonal into thick slices, and arrange on the warmed dinner plates. Spoon the sauce over the duck slices, and arrange the figs alongside. Serve.

WINE SUGGESTION: Almost any good southern Rhône red would be perfect here. Cassis is an overriding flavor in the wines of the region; try the Côtes-du-Rhône-Villages Cairanne from the Domaine de l'Oratoire Saint Martin, the Réserve des Seigneurs, loaded with the spice of red and black currants as well as kirsch.

VARIATION: Substitute cherries for the figs and cherry eau-de-vie for the *crème de cassis*.

NOTE: Leonardi brand balsamic vinegar can be found in Patricia's Pantry at my Amazon Store, accessed via the home page of www.PatriciaWells.com.

RABBIT WITH MUSTARD AND TARRAGON

~ 4 servings ~

Tender saddles of rabbit bathed in bright-flavored mustard and tarragon sauce is both an "at home" meal as well as festive. I've lightened up and modernized this bistro classic, one that deserves its place at everyone's table. Note that, generally, rabbit has the same cooking time as chicken.

EQUIPMENT: Toothpicks or butcher's twine; a large skillet with a lid; a 10-quart (10 l) pasta pot fitted with a colander; 4 warmed dinner plates.

4 very thin slices pancetta or bacon

4 saddles of rabbit, each about 5 ounces (150 g)

Fine sea salt

Coarse, freshly ground black pepper

2 tablespoons extra-virgin olive oil

1 bottle (750 ml) dry white wine

1/2 cup (125 ml) French mustard

1 2/3 cups (410 ml) light cream or half-and-half

1/2 cup (20 g) minced fresh tarragon leaves

8 ounces (250 g) dried Italian tagliatelle pasta

1. Wrap a slice of pancetta or bacon around each saddle of rabbit and secure it with a toothpick or butcher's twine. Season generously with salt and pepper. In a large skillet, heat the oil over moderate heat until hot but not smoking. Brown the rabbit on all sides until well seared, about 8 minutes total. Transfer the rabbit to a platter. Wipe out the skillet.

2. Pour the wine into the skillet. Bring the wine to a boil and boil for 3 minutes to burn off the harshness of the alcohol. Add the mustard, cream, and half of the minced tarragon. Cover, bring to a simmer and simmer for 5 minutes. Taste for seasoning. Return the rabbit to the

sauce, cover the skillet, and simmer for 15 minutes. The rabbit should be moist, tender, and cooked through.

3. Transfer the rabbit to a platter. Remove and discard the toothpicks or twine. Tent the rabbit lightly with foil.

4. Meanwhile, bring 8 quarts (8 l) of water to a boil in the pasta pot. Add 3 tablespoons of fine sea salt to the water, add the pasta, and cook just until firm to the bite. Drain the pasta.

5. Add the pasta to the sauce, toss to coat the pasta, cover, and let sit for 2 minutes to allow the pasta to absorb the sauce. Transfer the pasta with a bit of sauce to the warmed dinner plates. Arrange a piece of rabbit alongside and spoon more sauce over the rabbit. Garnish with the remaining tarragon.

WINE SUGGESTION: I enjoy this with a southern Rhône white, the Côtes-du-Rhône Bouquet des Garrigues from domaine le Clos du Caillou. It's sturdy enough to stand up to the mustard and tarragon but likes the tender meat of rabbit and chicken.

THE SECRET: A fresh, newly opened jar of French mustard. Freshness is the secret here. A favorite brand is Edmond Fallot, from the town of Beaune. Fallot mustard can be found in Patricia's Pantry at my Amazon Store, accessed via the home page of www. PatriciaWells.com.

VARIATION: This is also delicious prepared with two skinless, boneless chicken breasts. Omit the pancetta, or grill or pan-fry it separately. Slice the breasts on the diagonal. Prepare the sauce, brown the breasts in a pan, and then add the poultry to the sauce and simmer gently for 10 minutes. Garnish with crumbled cooked pancetta.

I have a collection of antique holders for butcher's cotton twine, and though they are beautiful objects in the kitchen, they also have their practical side here, dispensing the twine to truss a chicken.

BRAISED CABBAGE WITH SMOKED SAUSAGE AND MUSTARD

~ 4 servings ~

This is my go-to winter weeknight dinner, an easy, four-ingredient main dish that warms the soul. I first sampled a version at a favorite Provençal restaurant, Le Pré de Moulin in Sérignan-du-Comtat. At first sight I thought the leaves of cabbage were giant ravioli; I love the trompe l'oeil quality of this dish. The shower of bright green minced chives tells us spring cannot be far away. As a variation, I sometimes add cumin or caraway seeds to the simmering stock. Be sure to open fresh jars of mustard for this dish—you'll want it fresh, fragrant, and pungent.

EQUIPMENT: 4 warmed, shallow soup bowls.

2 quarts (2 l) Homemade Chicken Stock (page 283)

About 1/2 head of green or white cabbage, trimmed, halved lengthwise, leaves separated

1 plump, coarse-textured smoked pork sausage, such as kielbasa (about 1 pound; 500 g)

Several tablespoons minced fresh chives

A variety of French mustards, for serving

1. In a large saucepan, bring the stock to a simmer. Add the cabbage leaves and braise, uncovered, over moderate heat just until softened, 10 to 15 minutes.

2. Meanwhile, fill a large saucepan with water and bring just to a boil. Add the sausage. Immediately turn off the heat and cover the pan. Let the sausage stand until firm to the touch and heated through, 10 to 15 minutes. Slice the sausage.

3. To serve, spoon the stock into the warmed bowls, add the braised cabbage leaves, and arrange the slices of sausage on top of the cabbage. Top with the chives and serve with the mustards.

THE SECRET: Fresh cabbage, of course. And braising the leaves, which gives them a mild and just slightly crunchy quality, a fine contrast to the soft and silken sausage.

WINE SUGGESTION: I never need an excuse to open a bottle of Domaine Ostertag's dry Alsatian Riesling, Vignoble d'E: refreshing, firm, dry, always a delight.

FRICASSÉE OF CHICKEN WITH FENNEL, CAPERS, ARTICHOKES, AND TOMATOES

~ 6 servings ~

Neither my family nor my students ever get enough of a good chicken fricassée. Walter is a master at cutting up a chicken—students love to watch—and a nicely cut-up chicken (versus one that's been "butchered") makes all the difference.

EQUIPMENT: A large, deep skillet or Dutch oven, with a lid.

1 farm-fresh chicken (3 to 4 pounds; 1.5 to 2 kg), preferably organic and free-range, cut into 8 serving pieces, at room temperature

Fine sea salt

Coarse, freshly ground black pepper

3 tablespoons extra-virgin olive oil

2 onions, peeled, halved, and thinly sliced

2 fennel bulbs, trimmed and thinly sliced

1 cup (250 ml) dry white wine

One 28-ounce (794 g) can diced Italian tomatoes in juice

1 cup (115 g) green Picholine olives, pitted

1 cup (115 g) brine-cured black olives, pitted

1/4 cup (60 ml) capers in vinegar, drained

12 artichoke hearts marinated in olive oil, drained

Cooked rice or fresh pasta, for serving

1. Liberally season the chicken on all sides with salt and pepper.

2. In the large, deep skillet, heat the oil over moderate heat until hot but not smoking. Add the chicken pieces (in batches if necessary) and brown until they turn an even golden color, about 5 minutes. Turn the pieces and brown them on the other side, 5 minutes more. Carefully regulate the heat to avoid scorching the skin. When the pieces are browned, use tongs (to avoid piercing the poultry) to transfer them to a platter.

3. Reduce the heat to low, add the onions and fennel to the skillet, and sweat—cook, covered, over low heat—until soft but not browned, about 10 minutes. Return the chicken to the skillet. Add the wine, tomatoes (with juices), olives, capers, and artichokes. Cover and simmer over low heat until the chicken is cooked through, about 30 minutes. Taste for seasoning. Serve with rice or fresh pasta.

WINE SUGGESTION: A regular house wine at our family table as well as in our classes is a Languedoc red, the Clos de l'Anhel Corbières les Terrassettes from Sophie Guiraudon and Philippe Mathias. It's a lively, spicy, peppery red that pairs well with this zesty chicken dish.

BEEF DAUBE WITH FRESH PASTA SQUARES

~ 8 servings ~

There is a story behind each recipe. This one has several. The last day of our last Provence class one September, I sent a student to the vegetable garden for salad greens and herbs. She came back screaming, "Your garden has been destroyed! Everything is in disarray!" Sure enough. Big chunks had been chewed from the pumpkins. Zucchini plants had been pulled out, lettuces trampled, there were crater-like holes everywhere. The wild boars had had a midnight party. I didn't cry because we were leaving the next day and wouldn't be back for several months. But I laughed when I saw that they had not touched the arugula or the *shiso*! No gourmets, those boars. Fast forward to Christmas: A neighbor who is a veteran hunter arrived at the door with a huge package of frozen wild boar, promising me that this was not the animal who had destroyed my garden. (How could he be sure?) I thought about re-gifting the creature but decided cooking it myself might be the best revenge. The daube was delicious.

Back in Paris, I decided to re-test the recipe with beef, and when I went to my local butcher and simply asked for 2 kg (4 pounds) of beef for a daube, preferably two or three different cuts, he created a veritable still life. I arrived home with three cuts of beef, strips of caul fat, marrow bones, and of course a garnish of fresh parsley! While the daube can be prepared with a single cut of meat, I like to use two or three to allow for more complex flavors and textures. Careful searing of the meat is essential to seal in the juices. Flaming the wine adds another layer of flavor. A few marrow bones and strips of caul fat add a fabulous, silken texture to the final product. And while most French daube recipes recommend using either fresh tagliatelle or dried penne pasta, I prefer sheets of fresh pasta. They're prettier on the plate, easier to eat, and more quickly absorb the silken sauce.

EQUIPMENT: A heavy-duty flameproof casserole with a lid or Dutch oven; a 10-quart (10 l) pasta pot fitted with a colander; 8 warmed, shallow soup bowls.

1/4 cup (60 ml) extra-virgin olive oil

4 pounds (2 kg) beef (see Note), cut into 3-ounce (90 g) pieces

Fine sea salt

Coarse, freshly ground black pepper

2 bottles each (750 ml) of full-bodied red wine, such as a Côtes-du-Rhône

2 quarts (2 l) Homemade Chicken Stock (page 283)

2 large onions, peeled, halved crosswise, and cut into thin rings

4 carrots, peeled and cut into thick rounds

4 fresh or dried bay leaves

2 tablespoons tomato paste

Several strips of caul fat (optional)

Several marrow bones (optional)

2 tablespoons (30 g) unsalted butter

1 pound (500 g) fresh mushrooms, cleaned, trimmed, and thinly sliced lengthwise

3 tablespoons freshly squeezed lemon juice

5 ounces (150 g) pancetta, rind removed, cut into matchsticks

3 tablespoons coarse sea salt

Eight 5-inch (12.5 cm) squares of fresh pasta

Fresh flat-leaf parsley leaves, for garnish

1. In the casserole, heat the oil over moderately high heat until hot but not smoking. Add several pieces of the meat and brown them over moderate heat, regulating the heat to avoid scorching the meat. Do not crowd the pan and be patient: good browning is essential for the meat to retain its flavor and moistness. Thoroughly brown the meat on all sides in several batches, about 10

minutes per batch. As each batch is browned, use tongs (to avoid piercing the meat) to transfer the beef to a platter, and immediately season the meat generously with salt and pepper. Return all the meat to the casserole. Add the wine and bring to a simmer. Light a long-handled match and dip it into the simmering liquid to burn off the alcohol and give the daube a deeper flavor. Be very careful here: be sure nothing flammable is near the burner. It will take about 4 minutes to burn off the alcohol.

2. Add the stock, onions, carrots, bay leaves, and tomato paste. If using, add the caul fat and marrow bones. Cover and bring just to a simmer over moderate heat. Cook, covered, maintaining a very gentle simmer, until the meat is very tender, 3 to 4 hours. Stir from time to time to coat the pieces of meat evenly with the liquid. The sauce should be glossy and thick. Taste for seasoning. (The daube can be prepared a day in advance, covered, and refrigerated. Reheat at serving time.)

3. Prepare the mushrooms: In a large saucepan with a lid, combine the butter, mushrooms, and lemon juice. Cover and cook over moderate heat until tender, about 5 minutes. Keep the mushrooms warm while finishing the dish.

4. Prepare the pancetta: In a large dry skillet, brown the pancetta over moderate heat until crisp and golden, about 5 minutes. With a slotted spoon, transfer the pancetta to several layers of paper towels to absorb the fat. Blot the top of the pancetta with several layers of paper towels to absorb any additional fat.

5. Fill the pasta pot with 8 quarts (8 l) of water and bring to a rolling boil over high heat. Add the coarse salt and the pasta, stirring to prevent the pasta from sticking. Cook until tender. Drain.

6. Remove and discard the bay leaves, caul fat, and marrow. Transfer a square of pasta to each warmed, shallow soup bowl. Arrange several pieces of meat and the carrots, onions, mushrooms, and pancetta on top of the pasta. Garnish with the parsley and serve.

   NOTE: Use two or three different cuts of beef here, choosing from the top or bottom round, heel of round, shoulder arm or shoulder blade, neck, or short ribs.

Here's a trick I learned from restaurateurs: After washing a wine carafe, fill it with cold water and let it sit for several days (or until the next use) and any residual stains should disappear.

To decant or not to decant? In our home, the answer is simple: Almost all wines (save for very, very old wines that might be fragile) benefit from decanting, anywhere from an hour to several hours ahead. The aeration and oxygenation actually "ages" the wine and opens it up, allowing it to express itself. This goes for whites as well as reds. In my cooking classes we often do a test, serving a decanted wine in one glass and wine from a just-opened bottle in a second glass. The decanted wine always wins with points on flavor and satisfaction.

LEMON-CURED SIRLOIN CARPACCIO

~ 6 servings ~

This Asian-inspired carpaccio is a nice change from the traditional Italian version. I love the citrus tang as well as the nice hit of fresh, fragrant herbs.

2 cups (500 ml) freshly squeezed lemon juice

1 tablespoon Vietnamese fish sauce, preferably Red Boat brand (see Note on page 56)

1 teaspoon fine sea salt

2 teaspoons sugar

1 teaspoon coarse, freshly ground black pepper

1 pound (500 g) beef sirloin, trimmed of fat and sliced as thin as possible

2 plump, moist garlic cloves, peeled, halved, green germ removed, and minced

1 large handful of fresh sawtooth coriander (*ngo gai*, also known as sawtooth herb; or a mix of cilantro, mint, and basil leaves), minced

1 fresh or dried red bird's eye chile, sliced

Vietnamese Dipping Sauce (page 293), for serving

1. In a bowl, combine the lemon juice, fish sauce, salt, sugar, and pepper. Stir to blend.

2. Arrange the slices of beef on a platter, pour the lemon mixture over them, and marinate for 10 minutes, being sure that the meat is thoroughly covered with marinade.

3. Remove the beef from the lemon mixture, and drain and discard the excess marinade. Carefully rearrange the slices of beef on the platter. Shower the meat with the garlic, herbs, and chile. Serve with the dipping sauce at the table.

SUGGESTION: A lovely chilled beer is in order here.

CHAR-GRILLED PORK PATTIES

~ 12 pork patties, 4 to 6 servings ~

Meatballs of any kind seem to be crowd-pleasers. This Vietnamese-inspired creation is wonderful served with the pickled vegetables and plenty of sauce for dipping the herb-rolled patties.

EQUIPMENT: A wood or charcoal grill.

1 pound (500 g) minced lean pork

4 shallots, peeled and cut into thin rings

8 thin scallions, white part only, finely chopped

4 lemongrass stalks (bottom third only), trimmed, outer leaves removed, and sliced paper-thin

2 plump, moist garlic cloves, peeled, halved, green germ removed, and minced

2 teaspoons coarse, freshly ground black pepper

1 tablespoon Vietnamese fish sauce, preferably Red Boat brand (see Note on page 56)

2 tablespoons grated fresh ginger

1 or 2 fresh or dried red bird's eye chiles, finely chopped

2 tablespoons vegetable oil

Vegetable Garnish

1 European cucumber, (1 pound, 500 g), halved lengthwise, seeded, and thinly sliced (do not peel)

1 large head soft-leaf lettuce, leaves separated

1/2 small bunch fresh sawtooth coriander (*ngo gai*, also known as sawtooth herb), leafy top portion only (or a mix of mint, cilantro, and basil leaves)

1/2 small bunch fresh mint leaves

1/2 small bunch fresh red *shiso* leaves (perilla, *tia to*) or mint leaves

Pickled Vegetables (recipe follows)

Vietnamese Dipping Sauce (page 293)

1. Place the pork on a large plate, and sprinkle with the shallots, scallions, lemongrass, garlic, pepper, fish sauce, ginger, and chile. With your hands, work the ingredients into the meat, distributing them as evenly as possible.

2. In a small skillet, fry up a spoonful of the mixture and taste it for seasoning.

3. Divide the pork mixture into 12 portions and form them into patties about 3 inches (7.5 cm) in diameter.

4. Prepare charcoal or wood for a medium-size fire in a barbecue grill. Let it burn until the coals glow red and are covered with ash. Thoroughly oil the grill, using a paper towel dipped in vegetable oil. Set the grill rack in place. (Alternatively, preheat a gas or electric grill.)

5. Brush the patties with vegetable oil and grill for about 8 minutes, turning them every 2 minutes, until cooked through.

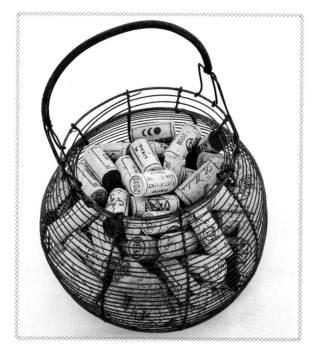

I never toss out a wine cork (meaning a real cork cork, not a plastic one). For one thing, I believe that they may not always be there, being replaced by the plastic or other noncork variety, and I want to keep them as a souvenir. On the practical side, they are great to use as kindling for fires. Just toss a handful in when starting a fire.

6. Arrange all the vegetable garnish ingredients on a large platter. Allow guests to help themselves to the cucumber and herbs, placing them on the patties before wrapping the patties in lettuce leaves. Serve with the Pickled Vegetables and Dipping Sauce alongside.

SUGGESTION: Beer is my beverage of choice here.

PICKLED VEGETABLES

~ Makes about 2 quarts (2 l) ~

2 large carrots, peeled and sliced into a fine julienne

1 small daikon (about 1 pound; 500 g), peeled and sliced crosswise into thin rounds

1 European cucumber, peeled, halved lengthwise, seeded, and sliced into thin half-moons

3 teaspoons coarse sea salt

1 cup (250 ml) Japanese brown rice vinegar, preferably organic

1/2 cup (100 g) superfine sugar

1. Place the carrots, daikon, and cucumber in three separate bowls. Toss each with 1 teaspoon of the salt. Let stand for 1 hour, tossing occasionally. Drain.

2. Place the vinegar and sugar in a large bowl and whisk until the sugar is dissolved. Add the drained vegetables and toss well. Let stand for 1 hour, tossing occasionally. (Store in an airtight container in the refrigerator for up to 2 weeks.) Drain before serving.

FOUR-HOUR AROMATIC STAR ANISE—BRAISED PORK

~ 10 to 12 servings ~

This fragrant pork dish fills the kitchen with spice and warmth as it braises long and slow in a warm oven. I like to prepare it a day in advance and reheat it at serving time; the flavors develop over time.

EQUIPMENT: A 6-quart (6 l) heavy-duty flameproof casserole with a lid or Dutch oven; a fine-mesh sieve.

3 pounds (1.5 kg) bone-in pork loin roast (do not trim off the fat)

Sea salt

Coarse, freshly ground black pepper

1/4 cup (60 ml) extra-virgin olive oil

3 tablespoons julienne of fresh ginger

24 small or 12 large shallots, peeled but left whole

12 plump, moist garlic cloves, peeled but left whole

6 whole star anise

1/2 cup (125 ml) Homemade Hoisin Sauce (recipe follows)

1 teaspoon honey

Sharp knives are essential, particularly for poultry and meats.

1. Center a rack in the oven. Preheat the oven to 275°F (120°C).

2. Lightly season the pork all over with salt and pepper. In a large, heavy-duty casserole that will hold the pork snugly, heat the oil over medium

heat until hot but not smoking. Add the pork and sear well on all sides, about 10 minutes total. Transfer the pork to a platter.

3. In the fat remaining in the casserole, combine the ginger, shallots, garlic, star anise, hoisin sauce, and honey. Cook over low heat until fragrant, 3 to 4 minutes. Taste for seasoning. Add 1 1/3 cups (330 ml) of water and cook for 2 minutes more. Return the pork to the casserole, bone side down.

4. Cover the casserole, place it in the center of the oven, and braise, basting about every 30 minutes, until the pork is just about falling off the bone, 3 to 4 hours.

5. Remove the casserole from the oven. Carefully transfer the meat to a carving board. Tent it loosely with foil and set it aside to rest for about 15 minutes.

6. While the pork is resting, strain the cooking juices through the fine-mesh sieve into a gravy boat, pouring off the fat that rises to the top. Discard the spices and vegetables. Serve the meat thinly sliced, passing the sauce.

WINE SUGGESTION: The Mas Champart Saint-Chinian from the Langeudoc takes well to this dreamy pork roast. The red wine is full of rich and smoky flavors that pair well with the spices and richness of the hoisin sauce.

HOMEMADE HOISIN SAUCE

~ Makes 1/2 cup (125 ml) ~

While testing recipes for our Vietnam classes, we found it impossible to find a good-tasting hoisin sauce that didn't contain a million additives, so we created our own.

EQUIPMENT: A small jar with a lid.

1/4 cup (60 ml) soy sauce, preferably organic

2 tablespoons peanut butter

1 tablespoon honey

1 tablespoon brown rice vinegar, preferably organic

1 plump, moist garlic clove, peeled, halved, green germ removed, and minced

1 teaspoon Sriracha sauce, or to taste

1/4 teaspoon coarse, freshly ground black pepper

In the jar, combine all the ingredients. Cover and shake to blend. Taste for seasoning. (Store in an airtight container in the refrigerator for up to 1 week. Shake again before serving.)

PASTA, RICE & BEANS

PENNE WITH TOMATOES,
ROSEMARY, OLIVES, ARTICHOKES,
AND CAPERS 138

FETTUCCINE WITH
VODKA AND LEMON 141

FRESH WHITE BEANS WITH GARLIC
AND BASIL-ARUGULA SAUCE 143

SPAGHETTI WITH ZUCCHINI
BLOSSOMS, ZUCCHINI, AND BASIL 145

SPAGHETTI WITH PECORINO
AND PEPPER: *CACIO E PEPE* 147

SPICY CHICKEN AND RICE PORRIDGE
WITH LEMONGRASS 150

GRILLED POLENTA WITH
TOMATO AND ONION SAUCE 153

OPEN RAVIOLI WITH MUSHROOMS 155

PENNE WITH TOMATOES, ROSEMARY, OLIVES, ARTICHOKES, AND CAPERS

~ 6 servings ~

There are evenings when I crave pizza but don't have the time to prepare it. That's when I turn to this pasta dish, one that has all my favorite pizza toppings turned into a sauce. Penne is the preferred pasta here, because it's sturdy enough to stand up to the rustic trimmings.

EQUIPMENT: A 10-quart (10 l) pasta pot fitted with a colander; 6 warmed, shallow soup bowls.

3 tablespoons course sea salt

1 pound (500 g) Italian penne pasta

2 cups (500 ml) tomato sauce or one 28-ounce (794 g) can diced Italian tomatoes in juice

1 tablespoon finely minced fresh rosemary

1/2 cup (60 g) best-quality brine-cured black olives, pitted and halved lengthwise

12 artichoke hearts marinated in olive oil, drained and cut into bite-size pieces

1/2 cup (60 g) capers in vinegar, drained

1 teaspoon fennel seeds

8 ounces (250 g) Italian whole-milk Mozzarella, cut into bite-size pieces

4 tablespoons fresh basil leaves, torn

Hot red pepper flakes, for serving

1. In the pasta pot, bring 8 quarts (8 l) of water to a rolling boil over high heat. Add the salt and the pasta, stirring to prevent the pasta from sticking. Cook until tender but firm to the bite.

2. Meanwhile, in a saucepan that is large enough to hold the cooked pasta, combine the tomato sauce or canned tomatoes, rosemary, olives, artichokes, capers, and fennel seeds. Simmer while the pasta is cooking.

3. When the pasta is cooked, remove the pot from the heat. Remove the colander and drain the pasta over the sink, shaking to remove the excess water. Immediately transfer the drained pasta to the sauce in the saucepan. Toss to evenly coat the pasta. Cover and let rest for 1 to 2 minutes to allow the pasta to thoroughly absorb the sauce. Taste for seasoning. Transfer to the warmed soup bowls, and garnish with the cheese and basil. Pass the red pepper flakes.

WINE SUGGESTION: A favorite household red is the inky-purple Vacqueyras, the southern Rhône wine from Domaine des Amouriers. Their Les Genestes is a typical blend of Grenache, Syrah, and Mourvèdre, with lots of spice that marries well with this pasta dish.

FETTUCCINE WITH VODKA AND LEMON

~ 6 servings ~

One of the greatest hits from my *Trattoria* cookbook was Penne with Spicy Tomato-Cream Sauce, or what is generally known as vodka pasta, a dish inspired by one served at a trattoria in Florence. This is a clear variation on the theme, made with nests of fettuccine and a nice hit of citrus. It's a real go-to weeknight pasta in our house.

EQUIPMENT: A 10-quart (10 l) pasta pot fitted with a colander;
a large skillet with a lid; 6 warmed, shallow soup bowls.

1 pound (500 g) dried Italian fettuccine

3 tablespoons coarse sea salt

1/4 cup (60 ml) freshly squeezed lemon juice

1/4 cup (60 ml) lemon vodka

1 cup (250 ml) light cream or half-and-half

1/2 cup (35 g) freshly grated Pecorino Romano cheese

Grated zest of 2 lemons, preferably organic

Coarse, freshly ground black pepper

1. In the pasta pot, bring 8 quarts (8 l) of water to a rolling boil over high heat. Add the fettuccine and salt, stirring to prevent the pasta from sticking. Cook until tender but firm to the bite, about 6 minutes. While the pasta cooks, warm the lemon juice, vodka, and cream in the large skillet.

2. When the pasta is al dente, remove the pot from the heat. Remove the colander and drain the pasta over the sink, shaking to get rid of the excess water. Reserve some of the cooking water for the sauce.

3. Add the drained pasta to the sauce and toss to evenly coat the fettuccine. If the pasta is dry, add pasta cooking water, tablespoon by tablespoon, until the pasta is moist. Add half of the cheese and toss once more. Taste for seasoning. Cover and let rest for 1 to 2 minutes to allow the pasta to thoroughly absorb the sauce. Toss again. Taste for seasoning.

4. Transfer the pasta to the individual soup bowls. Season with the lemon zest and freshly ground pepper. Serve immediately, passing the remaining cheese and a pepper mill at the table.

THE SECRET: The secret here is not to burn off the alcohol by reducing the vodka. Even though vodka is a neutral spirit, it is not flavorless. The key is that the flavor is in the alcohol, so burn off the alcohol, burn off the flavor.

WINE SUGGESTION: A lovely Italian white is my choice here. For some reason this dish takes me back to the charming town of Orvieto, so I'll suggest the Argillae Orvieto from Umbria.

FRESH WHITE BEANS WITH GARLIC
AND BASIL-ARUGULA SAUCE

~ 8 servings ~

This stunning summer vegetable dish appears often at our cooking school's Friday buffet. Fresh shell beans can be found in farmer's markets. When you spy them, buy as much as you can, shell the beans, and freeze them. They can be cooked directly from the freezer, without thawing.

1 tablespoon extra-virgin olive oil

10 plump, moist garlic cloves, peeled, halved, and green germ removed

2 pounds (1 kg) fresh small white beans in the pod, shelled, or 1 pound dried white beans

4 fresh or dried bay leaves

1 1/2 quarts (1.5 l) Homemade Chicken Stock (page 283) or cold water, or more if needed

1 teaspoon fine sea salt, or to taste

2 cup (250 ml) Basil-Arugula Sauce (page 289)

1. *For fresh beans:* In a large, heavy-bottomed saucepan, combine the oil and garlic and stir to coat the garlic with the oil. Place over moderate heat and cook until the garlic is fragrant and soft, about 2 minutes. Do not let it brown. Add the beans, stir to coat with the oil, and cook for 1 minute more. Add the bay leaves and the stock, and stir. Cover, bring to a simmer over moderate heat, and simmer for 15 minutes. Season with the salt. Continue cooking at a gentle simmer until the beans are tender, about 15 minutes more. Stir from time to time to make sure the beans are not sticking to the bottom of the pan. Add additional stock or water if necessary. Taste for seasoning. Remove and discard the bay leaves.

For dried beans: Rinse the beans, picking over them to remove any pebbles. Place the beans in a large bowl, add boiling water to cover, and set aside for 1 hour. Drain the beans, discarding the water. In a large heavy-bottomed saucepan, combine the olive oil and garlic and stir to coat the garlic with the oil. Cook over moderate heat until the garlic is fragrant and soft, about 2 minutes. Do not let it brown. Add the beans, stir to coat with the oil, and cook for 1 minute more. Add the stock, and stir. Cover, bring to a simmer over moderate heat, and simmer for 30 minutes. Season with the salt. Continue cooking at a gentle simmer until the beans are tender, about 30 minutes more. Stir from time to time to make sure the beans are not sticking to the bottom of the pan. Add additional stock or water if necessary. (The cooking time will vary according to the freshness of the beans.) Taste for seasoning. Remove and discard the bay leaves.

2. To serve, stir the Basil-Arugula Sauce into the beans. Taste for seasoning. Serve.

SPAGHETTI WITH ZUCCHINI BLOSSOMS, ZUCCHINI, AND BASIL

~ 4 servings ~

Summer gardens and farmer's markets call out for this quick pasta dish, full of bright flavors and colors.

EQUIPMENT: A mini food processor or a standard food processor fitted with a small bowl; a large saucepan with a lid; a 10-quart (10 l) pasta pot fitted with a colander; 4 warmed, shallow soup bowls.

4 cups (1 l) loosely packed fresh basil leaves

1/4 cup (60 ml) extra-virgin olive oil

1 teaspoon fine sea salt

3 tablespoons coarse sea salt

1 pound (500 g) Italian spaghetti

1 1/2 pounds (750 g) fresh zucchini, trimmed and cut into a very fine dice

20 zucchini blossoms, cut into a chiffonade (4 cups/1 l, loosely packed)

25 best-quality brine-cured black olives, pitted and quartered

5 tablespoons capers in vinegar, drained

1 cup (100 g) freshly grated Parmigiano-Reggiano cheese, plus more for the table

1. Combine the basil, 3 tablespoons of the oil, and the fine salt in the food processor and puree.

2. In the pasta pot, bring 8 quarts (8 l) of water to a rolling boil over high heat. Add the coarse salt and the pasta, stirring to prevent the pasta from sticking. Cook until tender but firm to the bite.

3. While the pasta cooks, heat the remaining 1 tablespoon oil in the saucepan until hot but not smoking. Add the zucchini and cook for 1 minute. Add the blossoms and cook for 30 seconds more. Add the olives, capers, half of the cheese, and the basil puree, and stir to blend.

4. When the pasta is cooked, remove the pasta pot from the heat. Remove the colander and drain the pasta over the sink, shaking to remove the excess water. Reserve some of the cooking water for the sauce.

5. Immediately transfer the drained pasta to the sauce in the saucepan. Toss to evenly coat the pasta. Remove from the heat. Cover and let rest for 1 minute. Toss with the remaining 1/2 cup (40 g) cheese. If the pasta seems dry, add several tablespoons of the pasta water to moisten it. Serve in the warmed bowls, passing extra cheese for garnish.

SPAGHETTI WITH PECORINO AND PEPPER: *CACIO E PEPE*

~ 4 servings ~

Sitting on the terrace of the bustling Roman trattoria Dal Bolognese one sunny Sunday in May, I relished a version of this classic dish, pungent with freshly ground black pepper and enriched with a mixture of sheep's milk Pecorino cheese and Parmigiano-Reggiano. We were dining with our friends George Germon and Johanne Killeen, and George noted that this is one of the hardest pastas to get right, probably because it is so basic and appears easy. The pepper flavor should be dominant, but should not overwhelm the palate. We eat pasta at least once a week, and this is one of my go-to preparations, since it comes together in a matter of minutes and is such a thoroughly satisfying dish.

EQUIPMENT: A 10-quart (10 l) pasta pot fitted with a colander; 4 warmed, shallow soup bowls.

---

3 tablespoons coarse, freshly ground black pepper, preferably Tellicherry

2 tablespoons extra-virgin olive oil

2 tablespoons (30 g) salted butter

3 tablespoons coarse sea salt

1 pound (500 g) Italian spaghetti

3/4 cup (50 g) freshly grated Pecorino Romano cheese, plus extra for serving

3/4 cup (75 g) freshly grated Parmigiano-Reggiano cheese, plus extra for serving

---

1. Place the pepper in a large skillet over medium heat and toast it, shaking the pan, until fragrant, about 30 seconds. Add the oil and the butter and stir until the butter is melted. Remove from the heat.

2. In the pasta pot, bring 8 quarts (8 l) of water to a rolling boil over high heat. Add the salt and pasta, stirring to prevent the pasta from sticking. Cook until tender but firm to the bite. Remove the pasta pot from the heat. Remove the colander and drain the pasta over the sink, shaking to remove the excess water. Reserve some of the cooking water for the sauce.

3. Return the skillet to the heat. Add about 4 tablespoons of the pasta water to the oil mixture and stir to blend. Add the pasta and toss until it is evenly coated. Add the cheeses and toss until the pasta is evenly coated. If the pasta is dry, add more pasta water. Serve immediately, with additional grated Pecorino and Parmigiano on the side.

THE SECRET: Buy the best peppercorns you can find. I favor the highly aromatic Tellicherry pepper from Malabar, off the coast of India, and love its spiciness, hint of wood, and lingering scent. The berries are left on the vines a bit longer, so they develop a deep, rich flavor. The peppercorns from The Spice House (TheSpiceHouse.com) are fabulous and reliable. And do invest in a good pepper mill, one that will coarsely grind the peppercorns. I use a battery-powered Peugeot mill. Peugeot mills are readily available in gourmet shops or can be found in Items for a Dream Kitchen in Patricia's Pantry at my Amazon Store, accessed via the home page of www.PatriciaWells.com.

SPICY CHICKEN AND RICE PORRIDGE WITH LEMONGRASS

~ 6 servings ~

Like oh so many recipes, this fragrant dish lends itself to endless variations. Substitute brown rice for the white rice, sautéed mushrooms for the chicken, and end with a flourish of bright green peas or a handful of peanuts or cashews as a final garnish. I adore the fragrance of the kitchen as this dish simmers away, all warming and exotic.

EQUIPMENT: A 3-quart (3 l) saucepan.

2 quarts (2 l) Homemade Chicken Stock (page 283) or Vegetable Stock (page 285)

2 lemongrass stalks (bottom third only), crushed, outer leaves removed, sliced paper-thin

2 fresh or dried red bird's eye chiles, seeded and thinly sliced on the diagonal

1 tablespoon Vietnamese fish sauce, preferably Red Boat brand (see Note on page 56), or to taste

2 cups (350 g) long-grain jasmine rice, well rinsed

1 1/2 pounds (750 g) boneless, skinless chicken breasts, cut into bite-size pieces

1/2 cup (125 ml) Vietnamese Dipping Sauce (page 293)

1/2 cup fresh cilantro leaves, plus fresh cilantro sprigs for garnish

Fine sea salt

Coarse, freshly ground black pepper

1 lime, sliced into 6 wedges, for serving

1. Pour the stock into the saucepan and bring to a boil over high heat. Reduce the heat to medium-low, add the lemongrass and chiles, and simmer, covered, for 10 minutes. Season with the fish sauce.

2. Add the rice to the stock and simmer, partially covered, until it is cooked through, 7 to 10 minutes.

3. While the rice is cooking, marinate the chicken in the dipping sauce.

4. Add the chicken and marinade to the rice, stirring to distribute the chicken evenly in the rice. Cook for 10 minutes more, or until the chicken is cooked through and moist and tender. Add salt and pepper and taste for seasoning. Remove the lemongrass stalks. Serve the porridge in individual bowls, garnished with the cilantro sprigs and lime wedges.

MAKE-AHEAD NOTE: All the ingredients for this dish can be measured in advance, but the dish should be cooked at the last moment. The results should be porridge-like, not firm.

GRILLED POLENTA WITH TOMATO AND ONION SAUCE

~ 4 servings ~

This light, colorful vegetarian weeknight dinner is a favorite, inspired by my annual visits to my "boot camp," Rancho la Puerta in Tecate, Mexico. This soothing, comfort-food dinner knows few rivals, particularly in cold weather.

EQUIPMENT: A 1-quart (1 l) gratin dish; 4 warmed dinner plates.

3 cups (750 ml) 1% milk

1/2 cup (125 ml) light cream or half-and-half

1 1/2 teaspoons fine sea salt

1/2 teaspoon freshly grated nutmeg

3/4 cup (135 g) instant polenta

1/2 cup (90 g) freshly grated Swiss Gruyère cheese, plus extra for garnish

1 large onion, peeled, halved lengthwise, and cut into thin half-rounds

1/4 cup (60 ml) extra-virgin olive oil

One 28-ounce (794 g) can whole peeled Italian plum tomatoes in juice

2 fresh or dried bay leaves

Fresh flat-leafed parsley leaves, for garnish

1. In a large saucepan, bring the milk, cream, 1 teaspoon of the sea salt, and the nutmeg to a boil over medium heat. (Watch carefully, for the milk will boil over quickly.) Add the polenta in a steady stream, and stirring constantly with a wooden spoon, cook until the mixture begins to thicken, about 3 minutes.

2. Remove from the heat. Add half the cheese, stirring to blend thoroughly. The polenta should be very creamy and pourable. Pour it into the gratin dish. Even out the top with a spatula. Sprinkle with the remaining cheese. Let sit at room temperature for about 30 minutes to firm up. (Or store, covered and refrigerated, for up to 3 days.)

3. Prepare the tomato garnish: In a large skillet, combine the onion, 2 tablespoons of the olive oil, and the remaining 1/2 teaspoon sea salt and sweat—cook, covered over low heat until soft and translucent—about 5 minutes. With a large pair of scissors, cut the tomatoes in the can into small pieces. Add the bay leaves and tomatoes and their juices and cook, covered, over low heat for about 15 minutes. Taste for seasoning.

4. At serving time, heat the remaining 2 tablespoons oil in a large skillet until hot but not smoking. Cut the polenta into 8 even squares. Sear each square on both sides until golden, about 2 minutes per side. Transfer the squares to the warmed plates, stacking the second slice at an angle over the first. Spoon the sauce all over. Garnish with parsley and cheese.

WINE SUGGESTION: An inexpensive everyday dish suggests an equally fine but gently priced wine. A favorite is Michel and Stephane Ogier's La Rosine Syrah, a deep purple vin de pays from the hillsides north of the old Roman town of Vienne.

MAKE-AHEAD NOTE: Both the tomato sauce and the polenta can be prepared up to 3 days in advance, then covered and refrigerated separately. Reheat at serving time.

THE SECRET: When using canned whole tomatoes, use a scissors to cut the tomatoes into small pieces, making for a still chunky yet finer sauce.

OPEN RAVIOLI WITH MUSHROOMS

~ 4 servings ~

Mushrooms amaze me—they give so much for so little. One of the least expensive vegetables to be found in the market year-round, the common button mushroom is a treasure of flavor, texture, aroma. A good fresh mushroom needs little embellishment: Here I simply cook the mushrooms in a touch of butter and a squeeze of lemon juice, then bathe them in a sauce of reduced light cream and stock. Top the mushrooms with a sheet of pasta and a garnish of parsley, and you've got dinner on the table.

EQUIPMENT: A 10-quart (10 l) pasta pot fitted with a colander; 4 warmed, shallow soup bowls.

---

2 cups (500 ml) Homemade Chicken Stock (page 283) or Vegetable Stock (page 285)

2 cups (500 ml) light cream or half-and-half

1 tablespoon (15 g) unsalted butter

1 pound (500 g) mixed domestic or mixed wild mushrooms, cleaned, trimmed, and halved lengthwise

1 tablespoon freshly squeezed lemon juice

3 tablespoons coarse sea salt

Four 5-inch (12.5 cm) squares of fresh pasta

Fresh flat-leaf parsley leaves, for garnish

---

1. In a saucepan, combine the stock and cream and reduce by half over high heat, 20 to 25 minutes.

2. In a large saucepan, combine the butter, mushrooms, and lemon juice. Cover and cook over moderate heat until tender, 10 to 15 minutes. Add the reduced stock mixture, and stir to coat the mushrooms. Keep the mushrooms warm while finishing the dish.

3. Fill the pasta pot with 8 quarts (8 l) of water and bring to a rolling boil over high heat. Add the coarse salt and the pasta, stirring to prevent the pasta from sticking. Cook until tender. Drain.

4. Arrange the sauced mushrooms in the center of each shallow soup bowl. Drape a sheet of pasta on top of the mushrooms. Garnish with parsley and serve.

WINE SUGGESTION: I like white wine with my mushrooms: Try the simple, light, refreshing Picpoul de Pinet from Domaine Félines Jourdan.

MAKE-AHEAD NOTE: Prepare the mushrooms and sauce earlier in the day, combine them, and refrigerate. At serving time, warm them while the water boils for the pasta.

PARIS

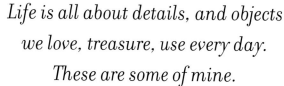

*Life is all about details, and objects
we love, treasure, use every day.
These are some of mine.*

Our good friend the writer Richard Reeves once said,
"Weather is Paris's best-kept secret." Meaning that from fall
to spring the days can be miserably dark and depressing.
And depressingly short. Another friend, the French cook
and teacher Lydie Marshall, offered one sage bit of advice
on looking for a Paris apartment: "Go for light!" The Paris
studio sucks up any light Paris has to offer, and the dining
table sits beneath a glass-covered roof. I love the play of
light on my blue and white kingdom.

It seems that all my life I dreamed of a home that was all
white and blue. I fulfilled my dream with my Paris cooking
studio, and find there is always an abundant selection of
blue and white kitchen objects for sale at flea markets to
fuel my fantasies.

Before the days of digital café bills, French cafés would set
a saucer before customers with the price of the item
ordered—a café, a croissant—imprinted with the amount
in French francs. The more customers ordered, the more the
saucers would stack up. The waiter would then just add up
the numbers on the saucers, and there was the total bill!

I have long had a passion for antique linens, and I don't
mind using items with someone else's initials. When
using well-worn tablecloths and napkins, I like to make
up names that match the monogram and think of all
the wonderful feasts they might have shared with family
and friends. Sometimes I even use linens with my own
monogram!

VEGETABLES

TOMATO *TATINS*

∼ 8 servings ∼

My good friend Jeffrey Bergman kindly shared this recipe with me one sunny day in August in Provence. We worked and worked on it (shucks, had to eat it *so* many times!) until we came up with this version, which we love. It is so fragrant and beautiful, and one of those *Did I really make this?* beauties.

EQUIPMENT: Three baking sheets; eight 1/2 cup (125 ml) ramekins; a 3 1/2-inch (8.75 cm) pastry cutter.

Tomatoes

3 pounds (1.5 kg) small, firm garden-fresh red heirloom tomatoes (about 15)

Fine sea salt

Extra-virgin olive oil spray

Pastry

A 14-ounce (400 g) sheet of Blitz Puff Pastry, well-chilled (page 294), or purchased all-butter puff pastry, thawed (see Note)

Shallots

4 large shallots peeled, halved lengthwise, and cut into thin half-moons

2 teaspoons extra-virgin olive oil

1/2 teaspoon salt

1/2 teaspoon ground *Espelette* pepper or other mild ground chile pepper

2 tablespoons red wine vinegar

Caramel

1/2 cup (100 g) white refined sugar (do not use dark unrefined cane sugar)

I always have a little spray bottle of olive oil at hand. It's convenient and practical for oiling pans, as well as for giving a last-minute "finish" or gloss to many dishes.

4 teaspoons water

1/8 teaspoon freshly squeezed lemon juice

16 fresh basil leaves, plus more for garnish

1/4 cup (25 g) freshly grated Parmigiano-Reggiano cheese

1. *Roast the tomatoes:* Center a rack in the oven. Preheat the oven to 275°F (135°C).

2. Core the tomatoes and halve them crosswise (at the equator.) Arrange the tomatoes, cut side up, side by side, on the baking sheet. Sprinkle lightly with salt. Spray lightly with oil. Place the baking sheet in the oven and bake until the tomatoes have shrunk by about one-third, 1 1/2 to 2 hours. This is an important step to condense the tomato flavor and reduce moisture. (The tomatoes can be baked up to 1 day in advance, stored in an airtight container, and refrigerated.)

3. *Prepare the pastry:* With the pastry cutter, cut out 8 rounds of pastry. Arrange the rounds side by side on a baking sheet. With a fork, prick the pastry. (The pastry rounds can be prepared up to 8 hours in advance. Cover and refrigerate.)

4. *Prepare the shallot mixture:* In a small saucepan, combine the shallots, oil, and 1/2 teaspoon of salt. Stir to coat the shallots with the oil. Sweat—cook, covered, over low heat, stirring frequently, until the shallots are soft and translucent—about 5 minutes. Add the *Espelette* pepper and the vinegar. Increase the heat to medium-high and cook until the vinegar has evaporated, but the mixture remains moist. Taste for seasoning. (The shallots can be prepared up to 1 day in advance, stored in an airtight container, and refrigerated.)

5. *Prepare the caramel:* In a medium saucepan, combine the sugar, water, and lemon juice and bring to a boil over high heat. Reduce the heat to medium and cook undisturbed until sugar begins to caramelize, about 1 minute. Pay close attention as the caramel will deepen in color quickly at this stage. Swirl the pan gently and cook until the caramel is a deep amber, about 1 minute more. Spoon a generous tablespoon of the caramel into the ramekins and tilt the ramekins so that the

caramel evenly coats the bottom. (This can be done up to 8 hours in advance. Store at room temperature.)

6. *Bake the* tatins: About 30 minutes before baking the *tatins*, center a rack in the oven. Preheat the oven to 375°F (190°C).

7. Arrange the caramel-coated ramekins side by side on a baking sheet. Place 2 or 3 tomato halves, cut side up, into each ramekin. Press down on the tomatoes so that they fit snugly into the ramekins. Spoon the shallot mixture on top of the tomatoes. Place 2 basil leaves on top of the shallots. Sprinkle with the cheese.

8. Place a round of chilled pastry on top of each ramekin and tuck the dough around the tomatoes. Place the baking sheet in the oven and bake until the pastry is puffed and golden and the tomatoes are bubbling around the edges, 25 to 35 minutes. Remove the baking sheet from the oven and transfer the ramekins to a rack to cool for at least 2 minutes.

9. Carefully invert each *tatin* onto an individual salad plate. Serve slightly warm or at room temperature, garnished with basil leaves. (The *tatins* can be prepared up to 8 hours in advance, stored at room temperature.)

THE SECRET: This dish offers a beautiful balance of sweet and acid. The shallots and vinegar, as well as the touch of caramel, are essential to creating a dish full of contrasting flavors.

NOTE: In our tests, we have preferred Dufour brand frozen puff pastry, available at most specialty supermarkets. See www.dufourpastrykitchens.com. Be sure to leave ample time for thawing frozen dough, at least 6 hours in the refrigerator.

PROVENÇAL LEMON-BRAISED ASPARAGUS

~ 4 servings ~

I adore asparagus and feel that this elegant vegetable best expresses itself when braised, bringing out an almost smoky flavor. Asparagus is so regal that I insist it stand on its own with the tiniest embellishment—here, a touch of lemon juice and zest.

EQUIPMENT: A large skillet with a lid; 4 warmed dinner plates.

1 tablespoon lemon olive oil or extra-virgin olive oil

16 plump spears (about 2 pounds; 1 kg) fresh green asparagus, trimmed

1 teaspoon coarse sea salt

Several fresh or dried bay leaves

Grated zest and juice of 1 lemon, preferably organic

Candied lemon zest, preferably organic, finely chopped

Fleur de sel

1. In a skillet that is large enough to hold the asparagus in a single layer, combine the oil, asparagus, coarse salt, and bay leaves. Sprinkle with enough water to cover by about one-third. Cover. Cook over high heat just until the oil and water mixture begins to sizzle.

2. Reduce the heat to medium and braise the asparagus, turning the spears from time to time, just until they begin to brown in spots, 6 to 8 minutes. (The cooking time will depend upon the thickness of the asparagus.) Shower with the lemon zest and juice.

3. Remove and discard the bay leaves. Transfer 4 asparagus spears to each of the warmed dinner plates. Shower with bits of candied lemon zest and season lightly with *fleur de sel.* Serve immediately.

THE SECRET: The words "serve immediately" mean business here: Once cooked, asparagus goes limp rapidly. Much of the joy of this preparation is the crunch of the just-cooked vegetable, so take advantage of it.

VARIATIONS: Substitute *yuzu* juice and *yuzu* zest for the lemon, or braise with the addition of either fresh mint or rosemary, removing the herbs once the asparagus is cooked.

In my kitchen, I like to have tools at hand, at eye level if at all possible. Here a selection of some favorite utensils—grater, mini whisk, apple corer, zester, egg separator, bread slashing knife—are within sight, within reach, making for a more efficient (and far less frustrating) time in the kitchen.

ASPARAGUS WRAPPED IN *COPPA* WITH PARMESAN AND PICHOLINE

~ 4 servings ~

Never too much asparagus in our home when the Provençal asparagus—green, white, and versions tipped with purple—are ready for braising or steaming, as here, wrapped with Italian charcuterie and paired with cheese and olives.

EQUIPMENT: Toothpicks; a steamer; 4 warmed dinner plates.

If I had to list ten of my favorite foods, asparagus and cherries would be among them. So, collector that I am, French faïence plates featuring those springtime ingredients are high on my collecting list.

16 plump spears (about 2 pounds; 1 kg) fresh green asparagus, trimmed

16 ultra-thin slices *coppa* or other cured pork, such as pancetta or Italian speck

1/4 cup (25 g) freshly grated Parmigiano-Reggiano cheese

1 tablespoon finely minced fresh rosemary

1 tablespoon extra-virgin olive oil

16 green olives, such as Picholine, pitted

1. Wrap each asparagus spear with a slice of *coppa* and secure it with a toothpick.

2. In a small bowl, combine the cheese and rosemary and toss to blend.

3. Bring 1 quart (1 l) of water to a simmer in the bottom of a steamer. Place the wrapped asparagus on the steaming rack. Place the rack over the simmering water, cover, and steam just until the asparagus give little resistance when pierced with a knife, about 8 minutes.

4. Heat the oil in a skillet over moderate heat. When it is hot but not smoking, add the wrapped asparagus and cook just until the *coppa* begins to brown, 1 to 2 minutes.

5. Transfer 4 asparagus packets to each of the warmed dinner plates. Remove and discard the toothpicks. Evenly shower the packets with the cheese mixture. Scatter the olives alongside. Serve.

MISO-GLAZED EGGPLANT

~ 4 servings ~

One sunny Friday in May my assistant, Emily Buchanan, and I sat at the counter of the Left Bank Japanese restaurant Azabu, relishing a version of this incredibly simple and elegant first course. The eggplant had virtually melted and was soft enough to savor with a wooden spoon. This fragrant, forward-flavored dish makes a perfect main-course vegetarian offering and also pairs beautifully with a roasted leg of lamb. The two are often on the menu at the opening Sunday night meal of our cooking school in Provence.

EQUIPMENT: A small jar with a lid; a baking sheet.

2 tablespoons sake or mirin

2 tablespoons dark barley miso or brown rice miso

1 tablespoon grated fresh ginger

1 tablespoon Japanese brown rice vinegar, preferably organic

4 small, firm, fresh Asian eggplants (each about 8 ounces; 250 g), washed but not peeled

Extra-virgin olive oil spray

1 tablespoon dark sesame seeds, toasted

2 tablespoons finely minced fresh chives

1. Center a rack in the oven. Preheat the oven to 425°F (220°C).

2. In the small jar, combine the sake, miso, ginger, and vinegar. Cover and shake to blend.

3. Trim and discard the stem end of the eggplants. Halve them lengthwise. Lightly score the flesh in a crisscross pattern. Spray the flesh lightly with the oil. Brush the scored eggplant with the miso glaze. Place the eggplant halves, cut side down, on the baking sheet. Place in the oven and bake until the eggplant skin is soft and wrinkled, about 30 minutes.

4. Sprinkle the sesame seeds and chives on top of the glazed eggplant. Serve warm.

THE SECRET: Ultra-fresh, firm eggplants are essential here. Cooking the eggplant cut side down on the baking sheet allows the vegetable to roast, rather than steam, resulting in a soft texture and rich flavor.

WATERCRESS PUREE

~ 4 servings ~

Come winter, watercress is the green I rave about the most—in salads, simply blanched, as a pairing for all manner of winter fare, or just a vegetable dish all on its own.

EQUIPMENT: A 10-quart (10 l) pasta pot fitted with a colander; a blender or a food processor.

2 bunches watercress (each about 8 ounces; 250 g), rinsed and lightly stemmed

3 tablespoons coarse sea salt

Freshly grated nutmeg

Fine sea salt

1. Prepare a large bowl of ice water.

2. In the pasta pot, bring 7 quarts (7 l) of water to a rolling boil over high heat. Plunge the watercress into the boiling water and blanch, uncovered, until the leaves are wilted and the stems are soft, 2 to 3 minutes. Drain, and plunge the leaves into the bowl of ice water. Once cooled, drain thoroughly.

3. Transfer the watercress to the blender or food processor and puree. Season with nutmeg and salt to taste. Serve immediately, or transfer the puree to a medium saucepan and reheat at serving time. (The puree can be prepared up to 3 days in advance. Store in an airtight container in the refrigerator.)

All of my cooking areas have a trio of salts: coarse sea salt for blanching or cooking pasta, fine sea salt for baking and everyday seasoning, and fleur de sel for finishing a dish. In dishes such as this Watercress Puree, a final tasting and a final seasoning are always essential.

ZUCCHINI BLOSSOMS STUFFED WITH GOAT CHEESE

~ 4 servings ~

This summertime starter is as colorful as an August day, and just as welcome. I never get tired of dreaming up uses for my morning harvest of golden zucchini blossoms, and this recipe puts the fragile, delicate flowers to perfect use. I mix the best fresh goat's milk cheese with a touch of egg yolk and lemon zest and spoon the mixture into the blossoms. The blossoms are tied with a chive, then quickly steamed.

EQUIPMENT: A food processor; a demitasse spoon; baking parchment; a steamer.

8 ounces (250 g) fresh goat's milk cheese

1 large egg yolk, preferably organic and free-range

Grated zest of 1 lemon, preferably organic

Fine sea salt (optional)

12 freshly picked zucchini blossoms

12 sturdy fresh chives

1. In the food processor, combine the cheese, egg yolk, and lemon zest and process to blend. Taste for seasoning. Some cheese may be salty enough and need no additional salt.

2. With the demitasse spoon, spoon the cheese mixture into each blossom. Carefully close each blossom, twisting to close. Tie the open end of each blossom with a chive to hold the cheese in place.

3. Cut out a piece of baking parchment large enough to fit the steamer basket. Place the paper in the basket and poke holes in the paper. Bring 1 quart (1 l) of water to a simmer in the bottom of the steamer. Arrange the blossoms on top of the parchment paper. Cover and steam just until

the blossoms begin to wilt but still hold their bright yellow-orange color, just under 1 minute. Do not over-steam or the blossoms will turn soggy and lose their color. With a slotted spoon, transfer 3 blossoms to each of 4 salad plates. Serve.

MAKE-AHEAD NOTE: The blossoms can be stuffed up to 8 hours in advance, covered, and refrigerated.

WINE SUGGESTION: A summertime white such as the refreshing Côtes-du-Rhône Villages Rasteau blanc from Domaine des Escaravailles, a remarkably complex blend of some of my favorite white grapes: Roussanne, Marsanne, and Clairette.

ONION "CARBONARA"

~ 8 servings ~

Chef Michel Richard from Washington, D.C., inspired this incredibly easy and yet satisfying vegetable dish. It's a takeoff on the pasta classic, only here onions are treated like pasta. This is delicious, and destined to become a standard on all of our tables.

EQUIPMENT: A steamer.

2 pounds (1 kg) large sweet white onions, peeled

1/2 cup (125 ml) light cream or half-and-half

1 large egg yolk, preferably organic and free-range

4 ounces (125 g) pancetta, rind removed, cut into matchsticks (optional)

Fine sea salt

2 tablespoons freshly grated Parmigiano-Reggiano cheese

Coarse, freshly ground black pepper

1. Slice the onions crosswise into thin rounds. Separate the slices into rings. You should have about 8 cups (2 l) loosely packed onions.

2. Bring 1 quart (1 l) of water to a simmer in the bottom of the steamer. Place the onions on the steaming rack. Place the rack over the simmering water, cover, and steam until the onions are "al dente," about 5 minutes. Transfer the onions to a bowl. (The onions can be prepared up to 8 hours in advance. Store in an airtight container in the refrigerator. Bring to room temperature at serving time.)

3. In a small bowl, combine 1/4 cup (60 ml) of the cream and the egg yolk, and whisk to blend. Set aside.

4. In a large skillet with no added fat, brown the pancetta (if using) over moderate heat until crisp and golden, about 5 minutes. With a slotted spoon, transfer the pancetta to several layers of paper towels to absorb the fat. Blot the top of the pancetta with several layers of paper towels to absorb any additional fat.

5. In a skillet that is large enough to hold the onions, combine the pancetta (if using) and remaining 1/4 cup (60 ml) cream, and warm for 30 seconds. Add the onions, season with salt, and cook just until they are warm, 2 to 3 minutes. Off the heat, stir in the reserved cream mixture and the cheese. Taste for seasoning. Shower with plenty of freshly ground black pepper. Serve immediately.

ZUCCHINI "SPAGHETTI" WITH GARLIC TAHINI DRESSING

~ 4 servings ~

I don't know when and where I first sampled this non-spaghetti, but I think it's a brilliant way to trick our minds into thinking we're eating pasta when it's really raw zucchini. I could live on this in the summer months, because the fine texture makes this light and oh so digestible. Be sure to follow to the letter the amount of salt: too much and the dish is inedible, too little and the zucchini will not give off enough of its liquid. The dressing is also delicious on roasted vegetables.

EQUIPMENT: A mandoline fitted with a julienne blade.

1 pound (500 g) fresh, small zucchini, rinsed, dried, and trimmed at both ends

1 teaspoon fine sea salt

1/4 cup (30 ml) Garlic Tahini Dressing (recipe follows)

Fleur de sel

1. Using the julienne blade of the mandoline, slice the zucchini into long julienne strips. Transfer the zucchini to a colander set over a mixing bowl. Toss the zucchini with the salt. Set aside for 15 minutes at room temperature.

2. Gently squeeze the zucchini to extract the excess water. Transfer it to a bowl and toss with just enough Garlic Tahini Dressing to coat the zucchini evenly. Season with *fleur de sel*. Serve.

GARLIC TAHINI DRESSING

～ Makes about 1 cup (125 ml) ～

EQUIPMENT: A blender or a food processor.

⸻

2 plump, moist garlic cloves, peeled, halved, and green germ removed

1/4 cup (60 ml) tahini (sesame paste)

1/2 cup (125 ml) whole-milk yogurt

2 tablespoons freshly squeezed lemon juice

1/2 teaspoon fine sea salt

⸻

In the blender or food processor, mince the garlic. Add the tahini, yogurt, lemon juice, and salt and puree to blend. Taste for seasoning. The dressing can be used immediately. (Store the dressing in a covered jar in the refrigerator for up to 1 week. Shake to blend again before using.)

BUTTER-BRAISED BABY POTATOES WITH CHIVES

~ 4 servings ~

This springtime specialty is a favorite in our Paris classes, where we usually pair it with roasted or steamed fish and of course asparagus for a colorful April palette.

1 pound (500 g) firm, yellow-fleshed potatoes, such Yukon Gold (each about 4 ounces; 125 g), scrubbed but not peeled

5 fresh or dried bay leaves

Fine sea salt

4 tablespoons (60 g) Clarified Butter (page 291)

4 tablespoons finely minced fresh chives

Fleur de sel

1. Place the potatoes in a large pot. Add the bay leaves, coarse sea salt, 3 tablespoons of the butter, and several tablespoons of cold water. Cover and cook over the lowest possible heat, turning them from time to time, until the potatoes are tender when pierced with a fork and are browned in patches, about 25 minutes. (The cooking time will vary according to the size and freshness of the potatoes.)

2. When the potatoes are cooked, transfer them to a bowl and toss to coat with the remaining 1 tablespoon butter and the chives. Season to taste with *fleur de sel* and serve.

EGGPLANT IN SPICY TOMATO SAUCE WITH FETA

~ 8 servings ~

Until I began growing eggplant, I had no idea how vibrant, smoky, and intense it could be, so fresh and firm, picked just seconds before preparation. Come August, my garden flourishes with those shiny black, lean and long vegetables, hanging from their neat little tree-like plants, ready for the oven, the skillet, the grill. I like to harvest them small, when I feel the flavor is more intense. This roasted eggplant buried in a spicy tomato sauce is a personal favorite, with multiple variations. I like to serve it as a vegetarian main dish, sometimes showered with cubes of Feta cheese and warmed just until the cheese begins to melt. The dish could also serve as a pasta sauce: chop the eggplant as it comes from the oven, then drop the cubes into the tomato sauce. Cumin, ginger, and pepper flakes have their place here as model partners to the versatile eggplant.

EQUIPMENT: A baking sheet; a large, deep skillet with a lid.

4 small, firm, fresh eggplants (each about 8 ounces; 250 g), washed but not peeled

2 tablespoons extra-virgin olive oil

1 teaspoon fine sea salt

2 onions, peeled, halved, and thinly sliced

6 plump, moist garlic cloves, peeled, halved, and green germ removed

2 tablespoons finely slivered fresh ginger

1/4 teaspoon hot red pepper flakes, or to taste

2 teaspoons ground cumin

One 28-ounce (794 g) can diced Italian tomatoes in juice

1 cup (125 g) Greek Feta cheese, cubed (optional)

1. Center a rack in the oven. Preheat the oven to 425°F (220°C).

2. Trim and discard the stem end of the eggplants. Halve them lengthwise. Brush the flesh lightly with some of the oil and season with the salt. Place the eggplant halves, cut side down, on the baking sheet. Place in the oven and bake until the eggplant skin is soft and wrinkled and the cut side is golden, about 30 minutes.

3. When the eggplants have almost finished cooking, prepare the sauce: In the skillet, combine the onions, garlic, the remaining oil, and salt. Toss to thoroughly coat the onions and garlic with the oil, and sweat—cook, covered, over low heat until soft and translucent—about 5 minutes. Add the ginger, pepper flakes, and cumin and toss to coat the onions evenly. Add the tomatoes (with juices) and simmer, covered, for about 5 minutes.

4. Add the roasted eggplant halves, burying them cut side down in the sauce. Cover and cook until the eggplant is very tender and has absorbed much of the sauce, about 20 minutes. If using, add the cubes of Feta cheese, warming the dish until the cheese melts. Taste for seasoning. Serve.

BRAISED FENNEL AND TOMATO STEW

~ 8 servings ~

I often pair this quick and easy stovetop vegetable stew with roasted leg of lamb, serving it at the opening Sunday night dinner of our cooking class in Provence. The dish lends itself to endless variations: leftovers can be pureed and turned into a lovely pasta sauce; one could add cubes of Feta cheese to turn it into a vegetarian main dish; or cubes of spicy sausage, such as chorizo, could add a touch of heat.

1/4 cup (60 ml) extra-virgin olive oil

2 large onions, peeled and quartered lengthwise

Fine sea salt

2 pounds (1 kg) fennel bulbs, trimmed and cut lengthwise into eights

6 plump, moist garlic cloves, peeled, halved, and green germ removed

1/2 cup (125 ml) dry white wine

One 28-ounce (794 g) can Italian peeled tomatoes in juice

1. In a large skillet, combine the oil, onions, and salt to taste. Sweat—cook, covered, over low heat—until soft but not browned, about 10 minutes.

2. Add the fennel, cover, and cook for 10 minutes. Add the garlic and wine and cook, uncovered, over moderate heat until the liquid is reduced by half, about 5 minutes. Add the tomatoes and crush to break them up. Simmer, uncovered, until the fennel is soft, about 30 minutes. Taste for seasoning. Serve warm or at room temperature.

WILD MOREL MUSHROOMS

~ 8 servings ~

I always have dried morels at hand, and love to prepare them in many ways. These can be served as a vegetable side dish or as a variation for Open Ravioli with Mushrooms (page 155) as well as Mushroom-Mushroom Soup with Chorizo Matchsticks (page 70).

EQUIPMENT: Dampened cheesecloth.

1 1/2 ounces (40 g; about 12 large) dried morel mushrooms

1 1/2 cups (375 ml) heavy cream or Homemade Chicken Stock (page 283)

2 teaspoons freshly squeezed lemon juice, or to taste

Fine sea salt

Coarse, freshly ground black pepper

1. Rinse the morels in a colander under cold running water to rid them of any grit. Transfer them to a heatproof cup or bowl and pour 2 cups (500 ml) hottest possible tap water over the mushrooms. Set aside for 15 minutes to plump them up. With a slotted spoon, carefully remove the mushrooms from the liquid, leaving behind any grit that may have fallen to the bottom, and set aside.

2. Place a piece of dampened cheesecloth in a colander set over a large bowl. Carefully spoon the soaking liquid into the colander, leaving behind any grit at the bottom of the measuring cup. You should have 1 1/2 cups (375 ml) liquid.

3. In a large saucepan, combine the strained morel liquid and the cream or stock and, uncovered, reduce by half over high heat, 15 to 20 minutes. Season to taste with the lemon juice, salt, and pepper. Add the plumped morels and heat until warmed through, 2 to 3 minutes. Serve.

EGGPLANT WITH CHICKPEAS, COUSCOUS, AND TOMATOES

~ 4 servings ~

During the last class of the week in Provence, always a Friday afternoon, we create a good number of vegetable dishes and set everything out on a table in the courtyard for a giant buffet. This fragrant, healthy dish is almost always on the menu.

EQUIPMENT: A serrated grapefruit spoon; a deep, ovenproof casserole; a very fine mesh sieve; a blender or a food processor.

4 small fresh, firm eggplants (each about 8 ounces; 250 g), washed but not peeled

2 tablespoons extra-virgin olive oil, plus extra for brushing the eggplant

Fine sea salt

1/2 cup (100 g) instant couscous

1 tablespoon freshly squeezed lemon juice

4 plump, ripe tomatoes, cored and quartered

4 small onions, peeled, halved, and thinly sliced

4 plump, moist garlic cloves, peeled, halved, green germ removed, and minced

2 teaspoons ground cinnamon, preferably Vietnamese cassia

2 teaspoons cumin seeds, toasted and ground

1/8 teaspoon hot red pepper flakes

3 tablespoons fresh thyme leaves

1/2 cup (125 ml) minced fresh flat-leafed parsley leaves

1/2 cup (125 ml) chopped fresh basil leaves

1/2 cup (125 ml) cooked chickpeas

1/2 cup (125 ml) golden raisins

About 2 cups (500 ml) plain Greek-style whole-milk yogurt

◇◇◇

1. Center a rack in the oven. Preheat the oven to 375°F (190°C).

2. Trim the eggplants and cut them in half lengthwise. Using the serrated spoon, scoop the flesh from the eggplants, leaving about 1/4 inch (5 mm) of the flesh still connected to the skin. Finely chop the flesh and set it aside.

3. Place the eggplant halves, cut side up, side by side in the casserole. Brush with oil and season lightly with salt. Place the casserole in the oven and bake for 10 minutes to soften the eggplant.

4. Place the couscous in the very fine mesh sieve and rinse it thoroughly under cold running water. Place the couscous in a large bowl. Toss with a fork to blend. Set aside.

5. In the blender or food processor, combine the lemon juice and tomatoes. Process to blend. Pour the mixture into the bowl of couscous and toss with a fork to blend. Fluff until the grains are evenly separated. Cover and set aside, occasionally fluffing and tossing the grains until all the liquid has been absorbed, about 3 minutes.

6. In a large, unheated skillet, combine 1 tablespoon of the oil, the onions, garlic, and sea salt to taste. Sweat—cook, covered, over low heat until soft and translucent—about 3 minutes. Add the couscous with tomatoes, the cinnamon, cumin, red pepper flakes, thyme, parsley, basil, chickpeas, and raisins. Continue to cook, covered, at barely a simmer, for about 5 minutes.

7. In a medium skillet, combine the remaining 1 tablespoon oil and the reserved minced eggplant and cook, covered, over low heat until the eggplant is soft, about 5 minutes. Add to the couscous mixture. Cook for a few minutes more. Taste for seasoning.

8. Fill the eggplant halves with the couscous mixture. Cover the casserole with foil or a lid and bake until soft and bubbling, about 30 minutes. Serve warm, topped with the yogurt.

SMASHED POTATOES

~ 4 servings ~

These firm, golden potatoes are always a hit. With their crispy exterior and creamy interior, they allow the diner to experience the best of the potato. Potatoes are halved and steamed, smashed to flatten them, then seared with a touch of fragrant duck fat. A shower of salt and pepper and they're ready to go!

EQUIPMENT: A steamer.

I am told that these sturdy antique cast-iron pans come from Brittany, where they were used exclusively for cooking buckwheat crêpes and galettes over an open fire. I use them for everything, including Smashed Potatoes and Oysters Seared with Pancetta and Shiso.

1 pound (500 g) firm, yellow-fleshed potatoes, such Yukon Gold (each about 4 ounces; 125 g), scrubbed but not peeled, halved lengthwise

5 plump, moist garlic cloves, peeled, halved, and green germ removed

4 large fresh summer savory or thyme sprigs

2 fennel frond sprigs

2 tablespoons duck fat or unsalted butter

Fleur de sel

Coarse, freshly ground black pepper

1. Pour 1 quart (1 l) of water into the bottom of the steamer. Add the garlic, summer savory, and fennel sprigs and bring to a simmer over moderate heat. Place the potatoes, cut side down, on the steaming rack. Place the rack over the simmering water, cover, and steam just until the potatoes are fully cooked and can easily be pierced with the tip of a knife, 12 to 15 minutes.

2. Place a clean dish towel on a work surface, cover it with plastic wrap, and set the cooked potatoes on top of the plastic wrap. Spread another piece of plastic wrap over the potatoes. Smash each potato gently with the palm of your hand to burst it open. Each potato should still maintain its shape.

3. In a large skillet, heat the duck fat or butter over medium heat. Brown the potatoes until firm and golden, 3 to 4 minutes per side. Season with *fleur de sel* and pepper. Serve warm.

EGGS, CHEESE & FRIENDS

WALNUT BITES:
ITALIAN *PANPEPATO* 193

POTATO, CHEESE, AND BACON
GRATIN: *TARTIFLETTE* 196

WALTER'S BREAKFAST EGG 198

TRUFFLED *LE FOUGERUS* 200

SCRAMBLED EGG WHITES
WITH SPINACH AND MUSHROOMS 202

FRESH GOAT CHEESE TRIO 205

PARMESAN CRÈME BRÛLÉE 206

WALNUT BITES: ITALIAN *PANPEPATO*

~ Makes 32 bites ~

These crunchy walnut bites are rather irresistible. And versatile. A darker version of the Italian *panforte*, they offer a pungent, forward flavor, laced with freshly ground black pepper, cinnamon, cocoa powder, candied lemon peel, currants, and walnut halves. They are ideal to serve with a cheese course (a nicely aged Parmigiano-Reggiano and a sip of *vin santo* works for me), or team them up with a slice of the cheese, stack the two on a toothpick, and serve as an appetizer.

EQUIPMENT: A 9 1/2 x 9 1/2-inch (24 x 24 cm) baking pan; baking parchment.

1/2 cup (65 g) dried black currants or raisins

1/2 cup (120 ml) sweet wine, such as marsala, *vin santo*, or port

2 tablespoons (1 ounce; 30 g) unsalted butter

3/4 cup (150 g) unrefined cane sugar, preferably organic, vanilla scented (see Note)

1/4 cup (60 ml) intensely flavored honey, such as chestnut

1/2 teaspoon fine sea salt

2 cups (250 g) walnut halves

3 dried figs, stems removed, chopped

1 cup (90 g) candied lemon peel, preferably organic, cut into fine cubes

1/4 cup (40 g) unbleached, all-purpose flour

1 teaspoon coarse, freshly ground black pepper

1 tablespoon plus 1 teaspoon unsweetened cocoa powder

1 teaspoon ground cinnamon, preferably Vietnamese cassia

1. In a small bowl, soak the currants or raisins in 1/4 cup (60 ml) of the wine for 1 hour.

2. Line the baking pan with baking parchment, letting the parchment hang over the ends. (This will make it easier to remove the *panpepato* once it's baked.)

3. Center a rack in the oven. Preheat the oven to 350°F (175°C).

4. In a small saucepan, melt the butter over low heat. Add the sugar, honey, and salt, heating just until blended.

5. In a large bowl, combine the currants and their soaking liquid, the walnuts, figs, and candied peel, and stir to coat the walnuts. In another bowl, combine the flour, pepper, cocoa powder, and cinnamon, and stir to blend. Add the flour mixture to the currant mixture, along with the

remaining 1/4 cup (60 ml) wine. Stir to evenly coat the walnuts. Add the butter mixture and stir again to blend evenly. The mixture will be very dense and sticky. Spoon the mixture into the parchment-lined pan and smooth it out with a spatula. (Note that the mixture will be a walnut brown as it is placed in the oven and turns dark, almost black, as it bakes.)

6. Place the pan in the oven and bake until bubbly, dark, and fragrant, about 35 minutes. The mixture will be sticky, but will firm up as it cools in the pan.

7. Once it has cooled, cut the *panpepato* into very tiny bites. (Store in an airtight container at room temperature for up to 3 weeks.)

WINE SUGGESTION: As an appetizer, I love these with a glass of Champagne. With the cheese course, try an Italian *vin santo*, a Sicilian Marsala, a Porto, or a French *vin doux naturel*, such as the Grenache-based Rasteau from the southern Rhône.

NOTE: To make vanilla-scented sugar: Flatten 1 or several moist vanilla beans. Cut them in half lengthwise. With a small spoon, scrape out the seeds and place them in a small jar; reserve the seeds for another use. Fully dry the vanilla bean halves at room temperature. Place the dry halves in a large jar with a lid, and cover them with sugar. Tighten the lid and store for several weeks to scent and flavor the sugar.

POTATO, CHEESE, AND BACON GRATIN: *TARTIFLETTE*

~ 8 servings ~

Tartiflette is a hearty, filling, and satisfying cold-weather, one-dish meal, a combination of potatoes, onions, bacon, and the extraordinarily nutty Reblochon, the fat disk of cow's milk cheese from the Savoy area of France. While the potato/cheese/onion/bacon combination has long been popular in the ski regions of France and Italy, the actual *tartiflette* was created by Reblochon cheesemakers in the 1980s in hopes of increasing consumption of their product. It worked, and the dish has become a cold-weather French staple since. The name derives from the Savoyard word for potato, *tartiflâ*. While an authentic *tartiflette* can only be made with Reblochon, one could substitute a whole Camembert, cut into two half-moons.

EQUIPMENT: A steamer; a 10 1/2-inch (27 cm) square baking dish.

2 pounds (1 kg) firm, yellow-fleshed potatoes, such as Yukon Gold

4 ounces (125 g) smoked bacon, rind removed, cut into matchsticks

1 large onion, peeled, halved lengthwise, and cut into thin half-moons

1 whole Reblochon cheese (or substitute Camembert)

Coarse, freshly ground black pepper

3 tablespoons crème fraîche or heavy cream

4 tablespoons minced fresh chives

1. Center a rack in the oven. Preheat the oven to 425°F (220°C).

2. Scrub the potatoes, peel them, and slice them into 1/2-inch-thick (1 cm) rounds. Bring 1 quart (1 l) of water to a simmer in the bottom of the steamer. Place the potatoes on the steaming rack. Place the rack over the simmering water, cover, and steam just until the potatoes are fully cooked, about 25 minutes.

3. In a large dry skillet, brown the bacon over moderate heat until crisp and golden, about 5 minutes. With a slotted spoon, transfer the bacon to several layers of paper towels to absorb the fat. Blot the top of the bacon with several layers of paper towels to absorb any additional fat.

4. In the fat remaining in the skillet, lightly cook the onion over low heat just until soft, about 5 minutes. In a bowl, combine the bacon and onions.

5. Arrange half of the potatoes in the baking dish. Top with half of the onion-bacon mixture. Arrange the remaining potatoes on top, followed by the last of the onion-bacon mixture. With the back of a spoon, even out the surface. Cut the cheese crosswise into two half-moons. Arrange the cheese on top. Season with pepper. Drizzle with the crème fraîche, and sprinkle with the chives.

6. Place in the oven and bake until the mixture is bubbly and the cheese has formed a thick golden crust, about 25 minutes. Serve immediately.

WINE SUGGESTION: I enjoy this with a light, bright white from the Savoy region. A longtime favorite is the 100 percent Roussanne from the vineyards of André and Michel Quenard, their Chignin-Bergeron Les Terrasses: crisp, stony, dry, and loaded with mineral richness.

I line my cheese trays with fresh fig leaves, adding local color and ambience to any festive gathering.

WALTER'S BREAKFAST EGG

~ 1 serving ~

Simplicity is everything, and in this recipe so is immediacy. My husband makes two of these for our breakfast almost every morning. It takes just one to two minutes, and the result is delicious. Variations are unlimited: any kind of leftover vegetables, meat, or poultry can be folded into the whisked egg, along with seasonings such as fresh herbs, curry powder, hot pepper flakes, or hot sauce.

EQUIPMENT: A 1/2-cup (125 ml) ovenproof ramekin; a microwave oven.

1/4 teaspoon unsalted butter

1 large, ultra-fresh egg, preferably organic and free-range

Toasted sourdough bread, for serving (optional)

Fine sea salt

Coarse, freshly ground black pepper

1. Lightly butter the bottom and sides of the ramekin. Break the egg into it and whisk thoroughly with a fork. Place in the microwave and cover with plastic wrap. Cook at medium power for 50 to 70 seconds, depending on the oven and your desired degree of doneness. We like our whites plump and moist, and the yolks slightly set but still runny.

2. Serve on the toast, or beside it, or all by itself. Season with salt and pepper to taste.

   NOTE: Cooking more eggs at the same time in the microwave will take longer.

TRUFFLED *LE FOUGERUS*

~ 12 servings ~

Le Fougerus, an artisanal cow's milk cheese that belongs to the Brie group, has been a favorite of mine for decades. Supple, sweet, and salty, it's a perfect match for the fragrant black truffle, which loves to infuse itself into the flavors of this elegant cheese. *Le Fougerus* was once made on farms for family consumption, topped with a fresh fern leaf for decoration and a slightly woodsy flavor. About 6 inches (15 cm) round and 2 inches (5 cm) high, this raw-milk cheese is generally aged for about 4 weeks. A worthy substitute is the more ubiquitous full-fat cow's milk Brillat-Savarin, a cheese created in the 1930s by the dean of French cheeses, Henri Androuët. Brillat-Savarin is a bit thicker and fatter than *Le Fougerus* but is just as friendly to truffles.

EQUIPMENT: A small jar with lid; a mandoline or a very sharp knife; unflavored dental floss or a very sharp knife.

2 fresh black truffles (about 1 ounce; 30 g each)

1 *Le Fougerus* or Brillat-Savarin cow's milk cheese (a little more than 1 pound; 650 g), well chilled

1. With a vegetable peeler, peel the truffles. Mince the truffle peelings, place them in the jar, and tighten the lid. With the mandoline or very sharp knife, cut the truffles into very thin slices. Each truffle should yield about 20 slices.

2. With the dental floss or very sharp knife, carefully slice the cheese horizontally into 2 even disks, like a layer cake. Layer the truffle slices on top of the lower half of the cheese, and then reconstruct the cheese by adding the top slice. Wrap it securely in plastic wrap. Refrigerate for 24 to 48 hours to perfume the cheese with the truffles.

3. To serve, remove the cheese from the refrigerator and let it come to room temperature. Unwrap and place it on a cheese tray. Sprinkle with the minced truffle peelings. Serve, cutting the cheese into thin wedges.

WINE SUGGESTION: The last time we prepared this for our January Truffle Extravaganza, we savored the cheese with sips of Yves Cuilleron's Saint-Joseph Lyseras, a Marsanne-Roussane blend with plenty of acidity and matching minerality.

Multiple varieties of purple and white grapes grace our farm, and in season a bowlful is always found at the table with the cheese course, most often a collection of local goat's milk cheeses.

SCRAMBLED EGG WHITES WITH
SPINACH AND MUSHROOMS

~ 2 servings ~

Whenever I end up with an excess of egg whites, I turn to this quick and simple dish, made in a matter of minutes and always welcome at our table. Walter is the egg master in our house, and this method of starting the eggs in a cold pan, and simply stirring and stirring, has been dubbed by one student the "cold fusion" method. Depending upon what I might have in the refrigerator, I may also add an egg yolk, a whole egg, or some grated cheese.

EQUIPMENT: A large, nonstick skillet; a sieve; a 10-inch
(25 cm) nonstick crepe pan; 2 warmed salad plates.

2 teaspoons extra-virgin olive oil

6 large fresh mushrooms, cleaned, trimmed, and thinly sliced

Fine sea salt

8 ounces (250 g) fresh spinach, stemmed and chopped

Freshly grated nutmeg

6 large, ultra-fresh egg whites, preferably organic and free-range, at room temperature

2 slices Saffron and Honey Brioche (page 228), toasted and buttered, for serving

1. In the nonstick skillet, heat 1 teaspoon of the oil over moderate heat. Add the mushrooms, season lightly with salt, and cook just until soft, 3 to 4 minutes. With a slotted spoon, transfer the mushrooms to the sieve to drain. Add the spinach and 2 tablespoons of water to the skillet. Cover and cook until wilted, 1 to 2 minutes. Drain the spinach, and season with salt and nutmeg.

2. Pour the egg whites into a bowl. Very lightly beat with a fork (not a whisk, which would make the eggs dry out). Stir in the mushrooms and the spinach.

3. Warm the crepe pan for a few seconds over high heat. Add the remaining 1 teaspoon oil and swirl to evenly coat the pan. Pour the mixture into the crepe pan. Cook over medium heat, stirring gently but constantly with a wooden spoon until the mixture forms a compact mass. Do not overcook. The entire process should take about 4 minutes. Taste for seasoning. With a large spoon, transfer the mixture to the warmed plates. Serve with the toasted brioche.

WINE SUGGESTION: A sip of a light white is what I love here. A house favorite is the Languedoc white, Domaine Saint Martin de la Garrigue, a blend of Marsanne and Grenache Blanc, along with a touch of Viognier, Roussanne, Picpoul, and Terret: complex, ripe, with hints of fresh herbs.

Mise en place—*arranging all the recipe's ingredients— is an essential part of the cooking school experience, as well as a daily habit in my kitchen. I prefer to set my* mise en place *on a tray, which really helps to keep the kitchen neater. I save egg cartons to use as a handy container for arranging the eggs intended for any recipe.*

FRESH GOAT CHEESE TRIO

~ 8 servings ~

Cheese is on the table with nearly every meal in our classes. Sometimes it's a mixed selection of cow, goat, and sheep, at other times a regional selection from Provence, the Loire Valley, Normandy, or the Champagne region. But when I want just fresh goat cheese, I flavor a trio of young, fresh disks, using fresh herbs, spices, black pepper, or whatever appeals from the garden or the market.

6 tablespoons mixed fresh herbs (such as dill, tarragon, mint, and chives), finely minced

3 disks fresh goat's milk cheese (each about 6 ounces; 180 g)

About 1 tablespoon coarse, freshly ground black pepper

2 teaspoons Homemade Curry Powder (page 282)

1. Scatter the herbs in an even layer on a large plate. Roll one of the cheese disks in the herbs, completely coating the sides of the cheese. With your fingertips, press any remaining herbs into the cheese. Set the cheese on a plate or a platter.

2. Repeat the same process for the black pepper and the curry powder with the other 2 cheese disks. Serve immediately.

WINE SUGGESTION: The Loire Valley is goat cheese country as well as white wine country: what grows together goes together. Try Philippe Gilbert's delicate white Sauvignon Blanc Menetou-Salon from the Sancerre region. Chalky and dusty, it's a fine match for fresh young goat's milk cheese.

VARIATIONS: Toasted ground cumin; borage flowers and chives; whole black or yellow mustard seeds; ground turmeric; caraway seeds; cumin seeds.

PARMESAN CRÈME BRÛLÉE

~ 8 servings ~

Four favorite dairy products—eggs, cheese, milk, and cream—offer endless possibilities for variations. These custards are quick and easy to prepare, and can be cooked in advance. As they are, just broiled with a touch of additional cheese, they make a lovely luncheon dish with a tossed green salad. The preparation can be embellished by adding cooked wild or domestic mushrooms, black truffles, nuts, or bits of ham to the cheese before sprinkling it over the custards.

EQUIPMENT: Eight 1/2-cup (125 ml) ovenproof ramekins, egg coddlers, custard cups, teacups, or *petits pots*; a roasting pan.

1 1/4 cups (300 ml) light cream or half-and-half

1 1/4 cups (300 ml) 1% milk

1 cup (100 g) freshly grated Parmigiano-Reggiano cheese, plus additional for finishing

4 large, ultra-fresh egg yolks, at room temperature, preferably organic and free-range, lightly beaten

1. Center a rack in the oven. Preheat the oven to 300°F (150°C).

2. In a large saucepan, bring the cream and milk to a gentle simmer over moderate heat. Add the cheese and whisk to melt. Off the heat, whisk in the egg yolks.

3. Ladle the mixture into the ramekins.

4. Arrange the ramekins side by side in the roasting pan. Add enough hot water to the pan to reach halfway up the sides of the ramekins. Place the roasting pan in the oven and bake the custards until lightly set and pale golden on top, about 45 minutes. (The custards can be prepared up to 2 days in advance, covered, and refrigerated. Bring to room temperature at serving time.)

5. When you are ready to serve, arrange a rack in the oven about 3 inches (7.5 cm) from the heat source. Preheat the broiler.

6. Sprinkle the top of each custard with the additional grated cheese. Arrange the ramekins on a baking sheet. Place under the broiler and broil just until the cheese melts, 30 seconds to 1 minute. Serve.

WINE SUGGESTION: The simple elegance of this dish calls for a light yet rich white. I love Nicolas Melin's ripe Chardonnay, the Domaine la Soufrandise Pouilly-Fuissé Clos Marie. It's a crisp, all-purpose white that does not shout out but makes you aware, and loves the company of dairy.

BREAD & FRIENDS

PAN BAGNAT 210

MINI QUESADILLAS WITH
GOAT CHEESE AND LEMON THYME 214

MANCHEGO, CHORIZO,
AND PAPRIKA BREAD 216

THIN-CRUST PIZZA
WITH MOZZARELLA, ARTICHOKES,
OLIVES, AND CAPERS 218

TOMATO AND MOZZARELLA
TARTINES 224

CRANBERRY AND WALNUT BREAD 225

SAFFRON AND HONEY BRIOCHE 228

PAN BAGNAT

~ 4 servings ~

When we acquired our farmhouse in Provence in 1984, our visits were generally limited to brief weekend getaways from Paris. The high-speed train got us there in under three hours, and for our Sunday night return to the city, a snack was essential. *Pan bagnat*, or "bathed bread," the traditional Provençal sandwich that can be found at every bakery and market in the region, became our standby. It's inexpensive, includes many of the local Provençal ingredients, travels well, and is a meal all on its own. I'd prepare the sandwiches on Saturday after going to the market, letting the *pan bagnat* "mature," tightly wrapped and weighted down in the refrigerator, until departure time the next day. Since I generally find sandwiches too dry, with too much bread in proportion to the filling, *pan bagnat* solves the problem. When properly made, this layered affair is moist, crunchy, and substantial. Think of it as a *salade niçoise* between slices of baguette, a healthy, filling sandwich that traditionally includes fresh tomato slices, canned tuna, hard-cooked eggs, fresh peppers, scallions, anchovies, and black olives. When preparing the sandwich, some of the crumb is scooped out of the bread, reducing the proportion of bread and making for a satisfying moist *pan bagnat*.

The original *pan bagnat* was popularized in Nice in the nineteenth century, when fishermen carried the sandwiches as late-morning snacks. At that time the sandwich contained inexpensive cured anchovies, but later it was "enriched" with more expensive preserved tuna.

Today there is even a committee (*Association pour la Défense et la Promotion de l'Appellation Pan Bagnat*) to fight against versions of the sandwich that veer off course.

The city of Nice has an official website (www.panbagnat.com) that lists the ingredients essential to an authentic *pan bagnat*: bread, tomatoes, local green peppers, baby fava beans, black Niçoise olives, anchovies or tuna, basil, salt, and pepper. The site also suggests ingredients that are not included in the official repertoire but are tolerated: hard-cooked eggs, vinaigrette, artichoke hearts from Nice, radishes, onions, and garlic for rubbing on the bread.

While the traditional sandwich is made with round, hard rolls (not soft hamburger buns), today it's generally prepared with a classic baguette. The best versions are overloaded with a filling that must be moist, bathing the bread to soften it. A quality *pan bagnat* is a messy affair, and the filling should fall out as you eat it, so make sure to supply plenty of napkins. No matter how it is made, *pan bagnat* serves as perfect picnic fare, made for traveling. To this day, the sandwich remains our favorite train snack, washed down with a few sips of our own red Côtes-du-Rhône, Clos Chanteduc.

EQUIPMENT: A serrated grapefruit spoon.

2 plump, ripe heirloom tomatoes (each about 4 ounces; 125 g), peeled, cored, and thinly sliced

Fine sea salt

1 baguette (about 8 ounces; 250 g)

A 7-ounce (200 g) can of best-quality tuna packed in olive oil (no need to drain)

1 red bell pepper, trimmed and cut into thin strips

2 scallions, white and green parts trimmed and cut into thin rings

2 large eggs, preferably organic and free-range, hard-cooked, peeled, and cut into thin crosswise slices

6 oil-cured anchovy fillets

10 best-quality brine-cured black olives, pitted and halved lengthwise

Coarse, freshly ground black pepper

1. Layer the tomatoes, slightly overlapping, on paper towels. Season them with salt and set aside to drain for at least 10 minutes.

2. Halve the baguette lengthwise. With the serrated grapefruit spoon, remove some of the crumb, being careful not to break through to the crust. (I place the reserved crumbs on a baking sheet, spray them with olive oil, and toast them to use as croutons in a salad.)

3. In a bowl, crumble the tuna to reincorporate the oil. Add the bell pepper and scallions, and toss to blend.

4. Layer the ingredients on the bottom half of the baguette in this order: tomatoes, tuna mixture, eggs, anchovies, and olives. Season with black pepper. Cover with the top half of the baguette. Wrap tightly in foil. Place the sandwich on a tray, cover with another tray, and weight it down with a heavy object, such as a cast-iron skillet or a brick. Refrigerate for at least 2 hours or overnight. At serving time, unwrap and slice. The sandwich should be moist and crunchy.

MINI QUESADILLAS WITH GOAT CHEESE AND LEMON THYME

~ 32 appetizer servings ~

I'm always on the lookout for quick starters and snacks, and this is an easy, satisfying appetizer or substantial snack that can be paired with a tossed green salad.

EQUIPMENT: A wood, charcoal, gas, or electric grill; a food processor; a demitasse spoon; toothpicks.

4 ounces (125 g) soft, fresh goat's milk cheese

1 large egg yolk, preferably organic and free-range

Grated zest of 1 lemon, preferably organic

1/2 teaspoon fresh lemon thyme leaves or regular thyme leaves

1/4 teaspoon fine sea salt

Eight 8-inch (20 cm) wheat or yellow corn tortillas, preferably without preservatives

1. Prepare a wood or charcoal fire. The fire is ready when the coals glow red and are covered with ash. Alternatively, preheat a gas or electric grill.

2. In the food processor, combine the cheese, egg yolk, lemon zest, thyme, and salt and process to blend. Taste for seasoning.

3. Cut each tortilla into quarters. With the demitasse spoon, place a spoonful of the cheese mixture onto the center of each tortilla quarter. Carefully fold the tortilla quarters lengthwise and, at the long open end, secure with a toothpick.

4. Carefully place the tortillas on the grill and grill for about 1 minute per side. Serve warm.

The pairing of fragrant, pungent fresh lemon thyme and fresh goat's milk cheese is a Provençal marriage made in heaven. Use the thyme to season Mini Quesadillas with Goat Cheese and Lemon Thyme.

MANCHEGO, CHORIZO, AND PAPRIKA BREAD

~ 1 loaf, 24 thin slices ~

This quick bread takes you on an instant trip to Spain. I love this sliced and toasted, with more cheese and chorizo on top as a welcome snack.

EQUIPMENT: A nonstick 1-quart (1 l) rectangular bread pan.

Oil, for oiling the pan

1 1/4 cups (180 g) unbleached, all-purpose flour

2 teaspoons baking powder

1/2 teaspoon fine sea salt

3 large eggs, preferably organic and free-range, lightly beaten

1/3 cup (80 ml) extra-virgin olive oil

1/3 cup (80 ml) plain whole-milk yogurt

5 ounces (150 g) Spanish *Manchego* cheese, cut into 1/4-inch (1/2 cm) cubes

2 ounces (60 g) Spanish chorizo, cut into 1/4-inch (1/2 cm) cubes

1 teaspoon hot Spanish paprika

20 pimento-stuffed green olives

1. Center a rack in the oven. Preheat the oven to 400°F (200°C). Lightly oil the bread pan.

2. In a large bowl, combine the flour, baking powder, and salt. Mix to blend. In another bowl, whisk together the eggs, oil, and yogurt. In a third bowl, toss together the cheese, chorizo, paprika, and olives. Add the egg mixture to the flour mixture and stir to blend. Add the cheese mixture and stir to blend.

3. Pour the batter into the prepared pan. Smooth out the top with a spatula. Place the pan in the oven and bake until the bread is firm and golden, 25 to 30 minutes. Remove from the oven and place the pan on a rack to cool. Once it has cooled, unmold the bread and serve it at room temperature, in thin slices.

VARIATIONS: Omit the cheese and chorizo and replace them with 1 tablespoon toasted ground cumin and 1 tablespoon toasted whole cumin seeds. Or, for Curry Bread, omit the cheese and chorizo and replace with 1 tablespoon Homemade Curry Powder (page 282).

THIN-CRUST PIZZA WITH MOZZARELLA, ARTICHOKES, OLIVES, AND CAPERS

～ One 13-inch (33 cm) pizza ～

Walter and I eat this pizza at home about once a week. It's about as quick, simple, and satisfying a pizza as one could imagine. At a favorite Paris hangout, Pizza Chic, the wood-oven pizza is topped with crushed canned tomatoes and Burrata, the fabulous Mozzarella cheese that is wrapped around whole cream. The Burrata is added as the pizza comes from the oven, since its creaminess would make for a topping that would be too moist. (If you are using fresh Mozzarella, add the cheese with the other toppings before baking.) At times we like to embellish the pizza bit, adding olives, artichokes, and capers. And I always pass red pepper flakes for those who like a hit of spice on the pizza. This thin-crust pizza will soften as it cools, so devour it hot from the oven!

EQUIPMENT: A baking stone; a fine-mesh sieve; baking parchment; a pizza peel.

One 14 1/2-ounce (411 g) can diced tomatoes in juice

1 ball (300 g) Instant, No-Knead Thin-Crust Pizza Dough (recipe follows)

20 best-quality brine-cured black olives, pitted and halved lengthwise

6 artichoke hearts marinated in olive oil, drained and quartered

2 tablespoons capers in vinegar, drained

8 ounces (250 g) Italian buffalo-milk *Burrata* or Italian Mozzarella cheese

About 20 fresh basil leaves, torn

Olive oil spray

Hot red pepper flakes, for serving

1. Place the baking stone on the bottom rack of the oven. Preheat the oven to 500°F (260°C) or the highest oven temperature.

2. Pour the tomatoes into the fine-mesh sieve set over a bowl. Crush the tomatoes with a fork. (Reserve the drained tomato juice for another use.)

3. On a lightly floured work surface, roll the dough into a 13-inch (33 cm) round.

4. Place a sheet of baking parchment on the pizza peel. Fold the dough in half and carefully transfer it to the parchment. Unfold the dough.

5. Evenly spread the crushed tomatoes over the dough. If using, evenly scatter the olives, artichokes, and capers over the tomatoes. If using Mozzarella, tear it into bite-size pieces and scatter them over the topping. Sprinkle with half of the basil.

6. Transfer the pizza, still on the parchment, to the baking stone and bake until the dough is firm and crisp and the top is bubbly, about 8 minutes. Remove from the oven. If using *Burrata*, tear it into bite-size pieces and scatter it over the topping, allowing the cream to drizzle over the pizza.

7. Spray the surface of the pizza lightly with olive oil. Scatter the remaining basil on top. Cut into 8 equal wedges and serve immediately, passing red pepper flakes at the table.

THE SECRET: Baking the pizza on a piece of parchment paper makes it easier to transfer the dough to the baking stone, preventing it from sticking to the pizza peel.

WINE SUGGESTION: A nice southern Rhône is what I love with this pizza. Try our own home-grown Côtes-du-Rhône Clos Chanteduc, a peppery blend of Grenache, Syrah, and Mourvèdre.

*Our major variety of olives, tanche, begin their lives as tiny flowers in the spring
and are harvested black and ripe come December.*

~ Two 13-inch (33 cm) pizzas, fougasses, or bread tarts ~

I think that most of us could eat pizza every day, and here I offer my instant, no-knead, thin-crust dough that is made in a matter of seconds. Preheat your oven and it will be ready as soon as the oven is hot! Since the dough is rolled out very thin, there is no need to let it rise. Finely ground "oo" flour is worth seeking out because it allows for a fine, crisp crust.

EQUIPMENT: A food processor.

Students are always surprised when I bring out these polenta (cornmeal) and flour dusters, practical tools for all uses, particularly bread, pastry, and pizza.

Weigh, weigh, weigh. In baking we want accuracy, and a scale can be a cook's best friend.

1 tablespoon extra-virgin olive oil

3 cups (420 g) unbleached, all-purpose flour, preferably "oo," plus extra if needed (see Note)

1 package (2 1/4 teaspoons; 5.5 g) instant yeast

2 teaspoons fine sea salt

1. In a cup with a pouring spout, combine 1 cup (250 ml) of warm water and the oil.

2. In the food processor, combine the flour, yeast, and salt. Pulse to blend. Add the liquid, tablespoon by tablespoon, through the feed tube, pulsing until just before the dough forms a ball. You may not need all the liquid. (If the dough is too wet, add a bit more flour. If it is too dry, add a bit more liquid.)

3. Transfer the dough to a clean work surface and form it into a ball. The dough should be soft. Divide the dough into 2 balls. (The dough can be used right away, or will keep, covered and refrigerated, for up to 4 days. Punch down the dough as necessary.)

NOTE: "oo" flour can be found in Patricia's Pantry at my Amazon Store, accessed via the home page of www.PatriciaWells.com.

TOMATO AND MOZZARELLA *TARTINES*

~ 2 servings ~

Even on a chilly wintry day in Paris, one can enjoy a touch of summer with Poilâne's delicious open-faced sandwich, or *tartine*, served at the Cuisine de Bar. In this version, the sandwich is layered lavishly with thick slices of tomato, silken Mozzarella, and a shower of fresh basil.

EQUIPMENT: A toaster; a baking sheet lined with baking parchment.

2 thick slices sourdough bread

1 large, plump ripe tomato, thickly sliced

4 ounces (125 g) Italian whole-milk Mozzarella cheese, torn into bite-size pieces

2 tablespoons fresh basil leaves, cut into a chiffonade

1. Arrange a rack in the oven about 3 inches (7.5 cm) from the heat source. Preheat the broiler.

2. Arrange the slices of bread side by side on the parchment-lined baking sheet. Toast the bread.

3. Arrange the tomato slices on top of the toasted bread. Arrange the cheese on top of the tomatoes.

4. Place the baking sheet under the broiler and broil just until the cheese melts, 30 seconds to 1 minute. Sprinkle with the basil, and serve immediately.

CRANBERRY AND WALNUT BREAD

~ 1 loaf, 24 slices ~

I am elated that dried cranberries are now easy to find, because their faint sweetness and moistness match perfectly with the crunch of chunky walnut halves. This bread is always on the opening-night menu for my cooking school in Provence, where it is served with a generous assortment of local goat's milk cheeses.

EQUIPMENT: A nonstick 1-quart (1 l) rectangular bread pan.

1 teaspoon best-quality walnut oil, such as Leblanc brand

1 1/2 cups (170 g) dried cranberries

1 cup (125 g) walnut halves

1 1/2 cups (210 g) unbleached, all-purpose flour

1/2 cup (125 ml) lavender honey or other mild, fragrant honey

1 teaspoon pure vanilla extract

2 large eggs, preferably organic and free-range, lightly beaten, at room temperature

1/2 teaspoon baking soda

1/2 teaspoon fine sea salt

1. Center a rack in the oven. Preheat the oven to 375°F (190°C). Brush the bread pan with the walnut oil.

2. In a large bowl, combine the cranberries, walnuts, and 2 tablespoons of the flour. Toss to coat the fruit and nuts with the flour. (The flour coating will help prevent the fruit and nuts from sinking to the bottom of the pan.)

3.	In another bowl, combine the honey, vanilla extract, and 3/4 cup (185 ml) of the hottest possible tap water. Whisk to blend. Add the eggs, baking soda, and salt and whisk to blend. Slowly add the remaining flour, stirring to blend thoroughly. The batter will be lumpy but will even out in baking. Add the flour-dusted cranberries and walnuts, and stir to evenly distribute them in the batter.

4. Pour the batter into the pan. If necessary, even out the top with the back of a spatula. Place the pan in the oven and bake until the bread is a deep, dark brown and a toothpick inserted into the center of the loaf comes out clean, 40 to 50 minutes.

5. Remove the pan from the oven and place it on a wire rack to cool. Once it has cooled, unmold the bread and serve it at room temperature, in very thin slices. (Store, wrapped in foil, at room temperature for up to 3 days.)

THE SECRET: Top-quality honey makes all the difference here. Honey not only enriches the flavor of this bread but also helps keep it moist.

SAFFRON AND HONEY BRIOCHE

~ Makes 2 loaves, about 16 slices each ~

I have rarely seen students so enthused and bursting with pride as when their airy brioche puffs to grandeur in the oven, arriving shiny and golden to the table just moments later. There is great triumph in baking perfection, and after a class, e-mails, photos, tweets, and Facebook notations attest to the students' prowess in the kitchen. In my kitchens, I use honey rather than sugar as a sweetener. The reasons are simple: honey just makes food taste better, and for us it's a homegrown product, produced from the bees that call Chanteduc and Provence home. When preparing this brioche, don't omit the saffron; infusing it in the warm milk dramatizes the intensity of these golden threads and adds an exotic flavor and aroma to the final product, not to mention the touch of color.

Note that you'll need to start the brioche several hours before you plan to bake it.

EQUIPMENT: A heavy-duty mixer fitted with a flat paddle; a dough scraper; two nonstick 1-quart (1 l) rectangular bread pans.

Sponge

1/3 cup (80 ml) whole milk, lukewarm

A generous pinch of best-quality saffron threads (about 1 heaping teaspoon, 30 to 40 filaments, or 0.3 g) (see Note)

1 package (2 1/4 teaspoons; 9 g) active dry yeast

1 tablespoon honey

1 large, ultra-fresh egg, preferably organic and free-range, lightly beaten

2 cups (280 g) unbleached, all-purpose flour

Dough

1/3 cup (80 ml) lavender honey or other mild, fragrant honey

1 teaspoon fine sea salt

4 large, ultra-fresh eggs, preferably organic and free-range, lightly beaten

1 1/2 cups (210 g) unbleached, all purpose-flour

12 tablespoons (180 g) unsalted butter, at room temperature

Egg wash

1 large, ultra-fresh egg, preferably organic and free-range, lightly beaten

1. *Prepare the sponge:* In the bowl of the heavy-duty mixer fitted with the paddle, combine the milk, saffron, yeast, and honey and stir to blend. Let stand until foamy, about 5 minutes. Add the egg and 1 cup (140 g) of the flour, and stir to blend. The sponge will be soft and sticky. Sprinkle with the remaining 1 cup (140 g) flour, covering the sponge. Set aside to rest, uncovered, for 30 minutes. The sponge should erupt slightly, cracking the layer of flour.

2. *Prepare the dough:* Add the honey, salt, eggs, and flour to the sponge. With the paddle attached, mix on low speed just until the ingredients come together, about 1 minute. Increase the mixer speed to medium and beat for 5 minutes.

3. To incorporate the butter into the dough, it should be the same consistency as the dough. To prepare the butter, place it on a flat work surface, and with the dough scraper, smear it bit by bit across the surface. When it is ready, the butter should be smooth, soft, and still cool—not warm, oily, or greasy.

4. With the mixer on medium-low speed, add the butter a few tablespoons at a time. When all the butter has been added, increase the mixer speed to medium-high for 1 minute. Then reduce the speed to medium and beat the dough for 5 minutes. The dough will be soft and sticky.

5. First rise: Cover the bowl tightly with plastic wrap. Let the dough rise at room temperature until doubled in bulk, about 2 hours.

6. Chilling and second rise: Punch down the dough. Cover the bowl tightly with plastic wrap and refrigerate the dough overnight, or for at least 4 hours, during which time it will continue to rise and may double in size again. After the second rise, the dough is ready to use.

7. *To bake the brioche:* Divide the dough into 12 equal pieces, each weighing about 2 1/2 ounces (75 g). Roll each piece of dough tightly into a ball and place 6 pieces side by side in each bread pan. Cover the pans with a clean cloth and let the dough rise at room temperature until doubled in bulk, 1 to 1 1/2 hours.

8. Center a rack in the oven. Preheat the oven to 375°F (190°C).

9. Lightly brush the dough with the egg wash. Working quickly, use the tip of a pair of sharp scissors to snip several crosses along the top of each pan of dough. (This will help the brioche rise evenly as it bakes.) Place the pans in the oven and bake until the brioche loaves are puffed and deeply golden, 30 to 35 minutes. Remove the pans from the oven and place on a rack to cool. Turn the loaves out once they have cooled.

THE SECRET: Top-quality honey makes all the difference here. Honey not only enriches the flavor of this brioche but also helps keep it moist.

NOTE: The brioche is best eaten the day it is baked. It can be stored for a day or two, tightly wrapped. To freeze, wrap it tightly and store for up to 1 month. Thaw, still wrapped, at room temperature. A reliable saffron source is The Spice House, www.thespicehouse.com.

PARIS

Graine blanche

Fleur de soufre

Guimauve

When people ask me why I love copper, I respond that I like to use things that will live longer than I will! More seriously, I love the way food reacts to a sturdy copper pan, and love its aesthetics. In the end, it's all about a respect for quality in equipment, as well as ingredients.

A sturdy stove that will also live longer than I will is an essential in my kitchens.

When restoring my Paris studio, in a building dating from the 1700s, I was looking for an old, flea market look. One Sunday morning at the marché aux puces I found an assortment of oak drawer fronts from a graineterie, a shop that sold seeds and grains. My cabinetmaker restored them to their original luster and we reinstalled the clean metal labels.

Walter likes to hold up a knife with a broken tip and say: "This used to be a knife. But don't throw it away! Now it can be used for what it was used for before it was broken. Now you can open tins with confidence that you won't break the knife tip! Just hope it wasn't expensive!"

Detail of Paris kitchen tiles.

DESSERTS

CHESTNUT HONEY SQUARES

~ Makes 32 squares ~

These rich honey squares satisfy with just a single bite. And they are so pretty once they come from the oven that you will proudly announce, "I made these!"

EQUIPMENT: A 9 1/2 x 9 1/2-inch (24 x 24 cm) baking pan; baking parchment; a food processor.

Pastry

3/4 cup (120 g) unbleached, all-purpose flour

1/2 cup (45 g) almond meal (see Notes)

3 tablespoons (35 g) unrefined cane sugar, preferably organic, vanilla scented (see Notes)

1/2 teaspoon fine sea salt

6 tablespoons (90 g) unsalted butter, chilled, cut into cubes

1 large egg yolk, preferably organic and free-range

1/2 teaspoon pure vanilla extract

Topping

4 tablespoons (60 g) unsalted butter

1 cup (80 g) sliced almonds

1/3 cup (30 g) candied orange or lemon peel, preferably organic, cut into tiny cubes

1/3 cup (65 g) unrefined cane sugar, preferably organic

2 tablespoons intensely flavored honey, such as chestnut

1/2 teaspoon pure vanilla extract

1. Center a rack in the oven. Preheat the oven to 400°F (200°C).

2. Line the baking pan with baking parchment, letting the parchment hang over the sides. (This will make it easier to remove the dessert once it's baked.)

3. Prepare the pastry: In the food processor, combine the flour, almond meal, sugar, and salt. Pulse to blend. Add the butter and pulse until the mixture resembles coarse crumbs. Add the egg yolk, vanilla, and 1 tablespoon of water. Pulse to incorporate. Add 2 to 3 tablespoons of water, tablespoon by tablespoon, through the feed tube, pulsing until just before the pastry forms a ball. You may not need all the water.

4. Turn the dough out into the prepared baking pan. Press the dough evenly onto the bottom of the pan. Place in the oven and bake until the pastry begins to brown around the edges, 12 to 15 minutes.

5. While the pastry is baking, prepare the topping: In a saucepan, melt the butter over low heat. Add the almonds, candied peel, sugar, honey, and vanilla extract. Heat just until the ingredients are incorporated.

6. Remove the pan from the oven and spread the almond-honey mixture evenly over the pastry. Return the pan to the oven and bake until the topping is a deep gold, 12 to 15 minutes.

7. Remove from the oven. Transfer to a rack to cool in the pan. Once it has cooled, remove from the pan and cut into 32 squares. (Store in an airtight container at room temperature for up to 3 days.)

NOTES:

· Almond meal (sometimes called almond flour) is made from whole, unblanched (skin-on) almonds. For this recipe, whole, unblanched almonds can be finely ground in a food processor. Do not over-process or you may end up with almond butter.

· To make vanilla-scented sugar: Flatten 1 or several moist vanilla beans. Cut them in half lengthwise. With a small spoon, scrape out the seeds and place them in a small jar; reserve the seeds for another use. Fully dry the vanilla bean halves at room temperature. Place the dry halves in a large jar with a lid, and cover with sugar. Tighten the lid and store for several weeks to scent and flavor the sugar. Use in place of regular sugar when preparing desserts.

VARIATION: Substitute dried black currants for the candied citrus.

ALMOND AND POLENTA COOKIE CAKE: *SBRISOLONA*

~ 40 servings ~

It means a lot to say that this will be one of the most delicious tastes and textures you will put in your mouth in a lifetime. I first sampled this sandy cookie/cake/snack/dessert in a lovely Italian country restaurant near Verona—Osteria della Valpolicella—one Saturday in March. The cake came as a surprising close to a splendidly modern lunch that included a pristine white ball of home-made cheese set atop the region's spicy *mostarda*; paper-thin slices of home-cured beef; a stunning risotto laced with wild herbs and greens from the mountains; and a slab of local cheese teamed up with a mound of wilted wild greens and a crisp slice of grilled bacon.

The recipe for this local specialty comes from Rosetta Gasparini, a fine cook who is part of the kitchen team at Villa Giona, owned by the Allegrini wine family. If you go into the town of Mantua, you will hardly find a shop window that does not display this buttery, crumbly, irresistible cake. Traditionally, it is sampled with a sweet local red wine such as Recioto, but it can also be served with a generous sprinkling of grappa. *Sbrisolona* is a rustic dessert, baked as a slab on a baking sheet and set on the table as one whole piece. Guests break off an end and enjoy it with a sip of sweet wine. I use salted butter for this cake because I find it brightens the flavors.

EQUIPMENT: A food processor; an 18 x 13-inch (40 x 32 cm) baking sheet lined with baking parchment.

8 ounces (250 g) whole unblanched almonds

2 1/4 cups (320 g) unbleached, all-purpose flour

7/8 cup (105 g) instant polenta

16 tablespoons (250 g) salted butter, melted

3/4 cup (150 g) unrefined cane sugar, preferably organic, vanilla scented (see Notes on page 238)

1 large egg, preferably organic and free-range

1/2 teaspoon pure almond extract

3/4 teaspoon fine sea salt

1. Center a rack in the oven. Preheat the oven to 350°F (175°C).

2. Set aside 10 almonds for garnish. In the food processor, coarsely chop the remaining almonds.

3. In a bowl, combine the chopped almonds, flour, and polenta. Toss to blend. Set aside.

4. In another bowl, combine the butter, sugar, egg, almond extract, and salt, and stir to blend. Add the dry ingredients to the liquid ingredients, and stir until the mixture is homogeneous. The texture should be like that of cookie dough.

5. Rub the dough between your hands and let it drop onto the baking sheet so that it covers the sheet without any spaces in between. Scatter the reserved almonds on top of the dough.

6. Place in the center of the oven and bake until deep golden and crisp, 20 to 30 minutes. Let cool before serving.

7. The crumbly almond cake is not cut with a knife but simply broken into pieces with your fingers. (The cake keeps well, and can be stored in an airtight container at room temperature for up to 1 week.)

RED FRUIT SOUP

~ 6 servings ~

This colorful red fruit soup can come to the table almost any time of year, since top-quality frozen berries are so easy to find these days. But of course that does not compare to the fun of going out to the garden or farmer's market to secure your own.

EQUIPMENT: 6 chilled, shallow soup bowls.

Sauce

1 1/2 cups (180 g) raspberries, preferably organic

1 1/2 cups (180 g) strawberries, preferably organic

3/4 cup (150 g) unrefined cane sugar, preferably organic, vanilla scented (see Note on page 238)

3 tablespoons freshly squeezed lemon juice

Fruit

1 3/4 pounds (875 g) red fruit (a mix of strawberries, raspberries, blackberries, and red and black currants), preferably organic

Fresh mint leaves, for garnish

1. *Prepare the sauce:* In a medium saucepan over moderate heat, combine the raspberries, strawberries, sugar, and 1 1/4 cups (310 ml) of water. Bring just to a simmer and cook for 5 minutes. Remove from the heat and stir in the lemon juice. Set aside to cool. (If the sauce is to be used soon, place it in the freezer to chill. The sauce can be prepared up to 8 hours in advance, stored in an airtight container, and refrigerated.)

2. Hull the strawberries and if large, halve them lengthwise. Arrange the red fruit in the soup bowls. Pour the cooled sauce over the fruit, garnish with the mint, and serve.

RUBY RHUBARB BARS

~ Makes 16 squares ~

Rhubarb—still known as "pie plant"—always reminds me of my childhood, because wherever we lived my mother was sure to plant rhubarb in the vegetable garden, ensuring a steady supply of this tangy vegetable for pies as well as sauces for spooning over vanilla ice cream. But rhubarb can be visually problematic, often losing its gorgeous ruby red color as it cooks. I think that I have found a solution: in these delectable bars the rhubarb is not precooked—it is cut into extra-thin slices so it cooks quickly as the bars bake, retaining its bright red color.

EQUIPMENT: A 9 1/2 x 9 1/2-inch (24 x 24 cm) baking pan; baking parchment; a food processor.

◇◇

Pastry

4 tablespoons (60 g) salted butter, chilled

1 cup (140 g) unbleached, all-purpose flour

1/3 cup (65 g) confectioners' sugar

Grated zest of 1 lemon, preferably organic

1/2 teaspoon fine sea salt

2 tablespoons plain nonfat yogurt

Topping

   3/4 cup (150 g) unrefined cane sugar, preferably organic, vanilla scented (see Notes on page 238)

   1/4 cup (40 g) unbleached, all-purpose flour

   4 large egg whites, preferably organic and free-range

   3 cups (300 g) thinly sliced red rhubarb stalks (about seven 10-inch; 26 cm)

1. Center a rack in the oven. Preheat the oven to 400°F (200°C).

2. Line the baking pan with 2 pieces of baking parchment, letting the parchment hang over the sides. (This will make it easier to remove the dessert once baked.)

3. Prepare the pastry: In the food processor, combine all the pastry ingredients and process to blend. The mixture should be soft and pliable.

4. Press the dough evenly into the bottom of the baking pan. Place the pan in the oven and bake until firm, about 12 minutes.

5. While the pastry is baking, prepare the topping: In a bowl, combine the sugar, flour, and egg whites and whisk to blend. Add the rhubarb and stir to coat it evenly with the egg white mixture.

6. Remove the pan from the oven and spoon the rhubarb topping over the warm pastry. Return the baking pan to the oven and bake until the topping is firm and golden, 35 to 40 minutes. Remove from the oven and let cool. Remove from the pan and cut into 16 squares. Serve at room temperature. (Store in an airtight container at room temperature for up to 3 days.)

LEMON LOVE NOTES

~ Makes 16 squares ~

Lemon Love Notes are a memory-lane recipe from my days as a new bride in the 1960s. This quick, easy, inexpensive sweet was always on the menu then, and it remains a favorite cookie-like dessert, especially when served with a golden lemon sorbet.

EQUIPMENT: A 9 1/2 x 9 1/2-inch (24 x 24 cm) baking pan; baking parchment; a food processor.

Pastry

4 tablespoons (60 g) unsalted butter, chilled

1 cup (140 g) unbleached, all-purpose flour

1/3 cup (65 g) confectioners' sugar

Grated zest of 1 lemon, preferably organic

1/2 teaspoon fine sea salt

2 tablespoons plain nonfat yogurt

Topping

3/4 cup (130 g) unrefined cane sugar, preferably organic, vanilla scented (see Notes on page 238)

1 tablespoon (10 g) unbleached, all-purpose flour

2 large eggs, preferably organic and free-range

3 tablespoons freshly squeezed lemon juice

Grated zest of 1 lemon, preferably organic

1/2 teaspoon baking powder

1 tablespoon confectioners' sugar, for dusting

1. Center a rack in the oven. Preheat the oven to 400°F (200°C).

2. Line the baking pan with 2 pieces of baking parchment, letting the parchment hang over the sides. (This will make it easier to remove the dessert once baked.)

3. Prepare the pastry: In the food processor, combine all the pastry ingredients and process to blend. The mixture should be soft and pliable.

4. Press the dough into the bottom of the baking pan and slightly up the sides. Place in the oven and bake until firm, about 12 minutes.

5. While the pastry is baking, prepare the topping: In a bowl, combine the sugar, flour, eggs, lemon juice, zest, and baking powder and whisk to blend.

6. Remove the pan from the oven and pour the lemon topping over the warm pastry. Return the pan to the oven and bake until the topping is firm and golden, 35 to 40 minutes. Remove from the oven and transfer to a rack to cool. While it is still warm, dust the top with the confectioners' sugar. Once it has cooled, remove from the pan and cut into 16 squares. Serve at room temperature. (Store in an airtight container at room temperature for up to 3 days.)

A final dusting of confectioners' sugar adds not only an aesthetic touch to any dessert but also a sweet, tender touch with each bite.

Vanilla sugar is an indispensable ingredient in my kitchen. It's not only fragrant and aromatic, it helps use up something that might otherwise be discarded. Once I have used a whole vanilla bean (extracting the flavorful seeds for use in a recipe), I dry the beans on a windowsill, and then combine them in a large glass jar with organic raw sugar.

FIG AND ALMOND TART

~ 8 servings ~

We have multiple varieties of fig trees on our property in Provence, and from June to October they offer an abundance of sweet fruits, some vibrant green, some green tinged with purple, and some almost black. My favorite variety is the small and delightfully sweet Ronde de Bordeaux, an ideal fig for tarts and jams.

EQUIPMENT: A 10-inch (25 cm) tart pan with a removable bottom; a rolling pin; a baking sheet lined with baking parchment; a blender or a food processor.

A 14-ounce (400 g) sheet of Blitz Puff Pastry (page 294) or purchased all-butter puff pastry, thawed (see Note)

1 cup (80 g) almond meal (see Notes on page 238)

5 tablespoons (75 g) unsalted butter, at room temperature

1/3 cup (65 g) unrefined cane sugar, preferably organic, vanilla scented (see Notes on page 238)

2 tablespoons (20 g) unbleached, all-purpose flour

1 large egg yolk, preferably organic and free-range

1 tablespoon fig jam

1 3/4 pounds (874 g; 35 to 40) small purple figs, stems trimmed

Confectioners' sugar, for dusting

Roasted Fig Sorbet (page 272), for serving

1. Fold the pastry in half, transfer it to the tart pan, and unfold it. Without stretching the dough, lift it up at the edges so that it naturally falls against the rim of the pan. With your fingertips, very delicately coax the dough onto the rim. There should be a generous overhang. With the rolling

pin, roll over the top of the tin, trimming off the overhanging pastry to create a smooth, well-trimmed shell.

2.   Center a rack in the oven. Preheat the oven to 400°F (200°C). Place the tart shell on the baking sheet.

3.   In the blender or food processor, combine the almond meal, butter, sugar, flour, egg yolk, and fig jam and process to blend. Transfer the almond mixture to the pastry shell. Smooth out the top with a spatula. Place in the oven and bake just until the pastry firms up and begins to brown and the almond mixture browns, about 10 minutes. Remove from the oven.

4.   Cut an X in the top of each fig and gently squeeze from the bottom to open the fruit like a flower. Arrange the figs, cut side up, side by side on top of the almond mixture.

5.   Return the tart pan to the oven and bake until the figs and the filling are dark and bubbly, 20 to 25 minutes. Remove from the oven and transfer to a rack to cool. While the tart is still warm, sprinkle the top with confectioners' sugar. After about 10 minutes, carefully remove the tart from the sides of the pan, leaving it on the pan base. Serve warm or at room temperature, cut into wedges, with the Roasted Fig Sorbet. This tart is best served the day it is baked.

THE SECRET: Ripe but not overly ripe figs, which tend to give up too much liquid and turn the pastry soggy.

TIP: Figs freeze beautifully. Treat them as you would berries: Arrange the whole fruit, stem side up, side by side on a baking sheet, and place in the freezer. Once frozen, transfer to a resealable plastic bag and freeze for up to 3 months. For use, thaw at room temperature.

NOTE: In our tests, we have preferred Dufour brand frozen puff pastry, available at most specialty supermarkets. See www.dufourpastrykitchens.com. Be sure to leave ample time for thawing frozen dough, at least 6 hours in the refrigerator.

INTENSE CHOCOLATE CUSTARDS WITH NIBS

~ 8 servings ~

No matter the season or the setting, this thoroughly satisfying dessert hits the spot. The serving size is intentionally small—all the better to savor the intense hit of chocolate. I like to serve this with chocolate sorbet alongside, also embellished with a touch of crunchy chocolate nibs.

EQUIPMENT: A double boiler; a baster; eight 1/4-cup (65 ml) vodka or shot glasses.

5 ounces (150 g) bittersweet chocolate, such as Valrhona Guanaja 70%

3/4 cup (185 ml) light cream or half-and-half

2 tablespoons (30 g) unsalted butter

Fleur de sel

About 1 tablespoon chocolate nibs (see Note)

1. Break the chocolate into small pieces.

2. In the top of the double boiler set over, but not touching, boiling water, heat the cream and 1/4 cup (60 ml) of water just until warm. Add the chocolate pieces, stirring until the chocolate is melted. Add the butter and stir to melt and combine. Spoon the mixture into the glasses. (I have found that if you use a baster to "pipe" the chocolate into the glasses, it is less messy.) Refrigerate until firm, about 20 minutes.

3. At serving time, sprinkle with *fleur de sel* and chocolate nibs.

MAKE-AHEAD NOTE: The custards can be prepared up to 3 days in advance, covered, and refrigerated.

NOTE: What are nibs? Chocolate nibs are pieces of cacao beans that have been roasted and hulled. Nibs taste faintly similar to roasted coffee beans. They have a great crunch, a slightly nutty flavor, and a pleasant touch of bitterness.

WINE SUGGESTION: I love to serve this treat with the chocolate-friendly, sweet Banyuls reserve wine from Domaine La Tour Vieille in the Languedoc. With its touch of spice, hint of chocolate, and overtones of raspberry, what could be a finer partner for a chocolate dessert?

CHOCOLATE, HONEY, ALMOND, AND FIG BITES

~ 36 servings ~

You can't ask much more of a dessert: these small bites are quick, easy, satisfying, and made with healthy ingredients—honey, chocolate, and dried figs. I love to keep these on hand so that, mid-afternoon, I can have a bite or two of these tasty treats.

EQUIPMENT: A food processor; 36 paper petit-four cases; a demitasse spoon.

4 ounces (125 g) whole unblanched almonds

2 ounces (60 g) bittersweet chocolate, such as Valrhona Guanaja 70%, chopped

3 tablespoons lavender honey or other mild, fragrant honey

Grated zest of 1 lemon, preferably organic

1/8 teaspoon fine sea salt

1/2 teaspoon ground cinnamon, preferably Vietnamese cassia

4 ounces (125 g) dried figs, stems removed, finely chopped

1. Toast the almonds: Place the almonds in a large, dry skillet over moderate heat. Shake the skillet regularly until the nuts are fragrant and evenly toasted, about 2 minutes. Watch carefully! They can burn quickly. Transfer the almonds to a plate to cool. (The almonds can also be toasted on a baking sheet in a 350°F; 175°C oven.) In the food processor, coarsely grind the cooled nuts. Do not over-process, or you may end up with almond butter.

2. Arrange the petit-four cases side by side on a tray.

3. In a small saucepan, combine the chocolate, honey, and 2 tablespoons of the hottest possible tap water. Heat over moderate heat just until the chocolate melts. Stir to combine. Remove from the heat. Stir in the zest, salt, cinnamon, figs, and almonds.

4. With the demitasse spoon, spoon the mixture into the paper cases, filling them about three-fourths full. Refrigerate for at least 30 minutes to firm up before serving. (Store in an airtight container in the refrigerator for up to 2 weeks.)

    VARIATION: Particularly for those who may have a nut allergy, the almonds can easily be replaced with raisins or dried black currants.

PAVLOVA

~ 10 servings ~

Is there a more perfect, more welcome dessert than Pavlova? Make it any time of year, varying the soft fruits according to the season.

EQUIPMENT: A heavy-duty mixer fitted with a whisk; a baking sheet lined with baking parchment.

◇◇

1 1/4 teaspoons pure vanilla extract

1 1/4 teaspoons cornstarch

1 1/4 teaspoons distilled white vinegar

5 large, ultra-fresh egg whites, preferably organic and free-range, at room temperature

1 2/3 cups (330 g) superfine sugar

1 cup (250 ml) heavy cream

1 pound (500 g) mix of tart fresh strawberries, raspberries, blackberries, and red currants, preferably organic

◇◇

1. Chill the mixer bowl and whisk in the freezer for at least 30 minutes. (This will help the egg whites beat to maximum volume.)

2. Arrange a rack in the lower third of the oven. Preheat the oven to 275°F (140°C).

3. In a bowl, combine the vanilla extract, cornstarch, and vinegar, and mix until smooth.

4. In the chilled mixer bowl, whisk the egg whites on low speed until frothy, gradually increasing the speed, until stiff peaks form. Be careful not to overbeat or the whites may begin to liquefy. Add half the sugar to the stiffened whites, a tablespoon at a time, whisking until the mixture becomes thick and satiny.

5. Add the vanilla mixture to the whites, and with a large spoon gently fold it into the whites, taking care not to knock the air out of the whites. Add the remaining sugar and fold it into the whites.

6. Spread half the meringue mixture on the baking sheet, forming a round about 8 inches (20 cm) in diameter. Pile the rest of the mixture onto the round to make a tall tower, slightly flattening out the top.

7. Place the baking sheet in the oven and bake until the meringue is beginning to turn golden, 1 to 1 1/2 hours. Try not to open the oven door while baking. Turn off the oven and leave the meringue in the oven to cool. A rush of cold air while the Pavlova is still warm can cause it to collapse. (The cooled baked meringue can be stored in an airtight container at room temperature for up to 2 days.)

8. In the bowl of the electric mixer, whisk the cream into soft peaks.

9. When you are ready to serve the dessert, pile the cream on top of the meringue and top with the fresh berries.

TIP: The meringue will begin to liquefy if left to stand, so be sure to prepare all the ingredients before whipping the egg whites. Bake as soon as the Pavlova is prepared.

VARIATION: To create individual pavlovas, preheat the oven to 350°F (175°C). Spoon large dollops of meringue, about the size of a small fist, onto the lined baking sheet. Reduce the oven temperature to 285°F (140°C) and bake the meringues for 20 minutes. Turn off the oven and leave the meringues in the oven to cool completely, preferably overnight.

FRESH GINGER SORBET

~ 8 servings ~

I am never without fresh ginger in my kitchen. Any time of year one can whip up this easy, refreshing sorbet.

EQUIPMENT: An ice cream maker; 8 ice cream bowls, chilled in the freezer.

3/4 cup (150 g) unrefined cane sugar, preferably organic, vanilla scented (see Notes on page 238)

1/3 cup (75 ml) freshly squeezed lemon juice

Coarsely grated zest of 2 lemons, preferably organic

3 tablespoons grated fresh ginger, with juice

1/8 teaspoon fine sea salt

2 tablespoons vodka (see Note)

---

1. Combine 3 cups (750 ml) of water and the sugar in a saucepan and bring to a boil over high heat. Reduce the heat and simmer just until the sugar is completely dissolved, about 1 minute.

2. Remove the pan from the heat and add the lemon juice, zest, ginger, salt, and vodka. Chill thoroughly.

3. Transfer the mixture to the ice cream maker and freeze according to the manufacturer's instructions. For best results, serve the sorbet in well-chilled bowls as soon as it is frozen. Do not re-freeze.

THE SECRET: Use the fine holes of a cheese grater (I like the Oxo brand) to grate the ginger. It does a great job and also collects the precious juices.

NOTE: Why vodka? Without the added alcohol, this sorbet would have a tendency to become icy. The alcohol doesn't freeze, resulting in a smooth and creamy dessert.

RASPBERRY-YOGURT SORBET

~ 8 servings ~

I do sometimes feel rather spoiled. While I am up in my gym most mornings in Provence, Walter is in the garden gathering every little berry that's ripe: raspberries, blackberries, red currants, black currants, gooseberries. When I come to breakfast, I need to decide whether I consume the berries now or save them for a sorbet. Most days, half make up breakfast, half get saved for the sorbet.

EQUIPMENT: A blender or a food processor; an ice cream maker; 8 ice cream bowls, chilled in the freezer.

2 cups (200 g) fresh or frozen raspberries, preferably organic

1/3 cup (65 g) unrefined cane sugar, preferably organic, vanilla scented (see Notes on page 238)

2 teaspoons cherry eau-de-vie or kirsch (optional)

1 1/4 cups (300 ml) Greek-style plain whole-milk yogurt

2 tablespoons Invert Sugar Syrup (page 75) or light corn syrup

Since childhood, when we had a huge raspberry patch in Milwaukee, raspberries have been a favorite fruit.

1. In a large, shallow bowl, combine the raspberries, sugar, and eau-de-vie or kirsch if using. Crush with a fork to blend. Set aside for 1 hour to let the fruit absorb the sugar and eau-de-vie.

2. In the blender or food processor, puree the raspberry mixture with the yogurt and syrup. Chill thoroughly.

3. Transfer the mixture to an ice cream maker and freeze according to the manufacturer's instructions. For best results, serve the sorbet in well-chilled bowls as soon as it is frozen. Do not re-freeze.

BLACKBERRY SORBET

~ 8 servings ~

Our blackberry patch offers pungent, tart fruit come June, just in time for students to enjoy them in this tangy sorbet.

EQUIPMENT: A blender or a food processor; a fine-mesh sieve; an ice cream maker; 8 ice cream bowls, chilled in the freezer.

---

1 quart (500 g) fresh or frozen blackberries, preferably organic

2/3 cup (120 g) unrefined cane sugar, preferably organic, vanilla scented (see Notes on page 238)

1 tablespoon vodka, raspberry eau-de-vie, or raspberry liqueur (optional)

1 cup (250 ml) Greek-style plain whole-milk yogurt

---

1. Combine all the ingredients in the blender or food processor and puree until smooth. Strain through the fine-mesh sieve to remove the seeds. Chill thoroughly.

2. At serving time, transfer the mixture to the ice cream maker and freeze according to the manufacturer's instructions. For best results, serve the sorbet in well-chilled bowls as soon as it is frozen. Do not re-freeze.

CANTALOUPE SORBET

~ 8 servings ~

A ripe, juicy melon emits the most intoxicating perfume. Even before the fruit is sliced open, it offers up its rich, pleasantly musky aromas. Choose a melon that feels heavy for its size, a sign that the fruit is dense and ripe. In Provence, the fashion is to offer melons that have exploded at the bottom—like a little volcanic eruption—a sign that they were ripened in the fields and not waterlogged in a greenhouse to give better weight. I like to sweeten this sorbet with a mild yet fragrant and distinctive honey, preferably lavender. For a truly creamy, almost fluffy sorbet, whip the mixture in the blender at the highest speed for a full minute.

EQUIPMENT: A serrated grapefruit spoon; a blender or a food processor; an ice cream maker; 8 ice cream bowls, chilled in the freezer.

One 2-pound (1 kg) ripe cantaloupe (to yield about 1 pound; 500 g fruit)

1/2 cup (125 ml) lavender honey or other mild, fragrant honey

1 tablespoon freshly squeezed lemon juice

2 tablespoons vodka (see Note)

1. Halve the melon. With the grapefruit spoon, remove and discard any fibrous pulp and seeds. Slice the halves into 4 wedges each. With a sharp knife, run the knife between the rind and the pulp, being careful not to include any green bits of pulp. Chop the pulp coarsely.

2. Transfer the melon pulp to the blender. Add the honey, lemon juice, and vodka and blend for a full minute, until creamy and smooth. Chill thoroughly.

3. At serving time, transfer the mixture to an ice cream maker and freeze according to the manufacturer's instructions. For best results, serve the sorbet in well-chilled bowls as soon as it is frozen. Do not re-freeze.

NOTE: Why vodka? Without the added alcohol, this all-fruit sorbet would have a tendency to become gritty. The alcohol does not freeze, resulting in a smooth and creamy dessert.

I love the specificity of life. Of course we all need special spoons for oysters, melons, and yes, as here, ice cream.

Some call these oyster spoons, some melon spoons. I love them with any nomenclature, and use them regularly for both!

PUMPKIN "PIE" SORBET

~ 8 servings ~

One autumn day when students were out in the vegetable garden harvesting herbs and salad greens, one gatherer brought in a bright orange pumpkin, a *potimarron*, and suggested we dream up a pumpkin pie sorbet. We did, and here it is.

EQUIPMENT: A blender or a food processor; an ice cream maker; 8 ice cream bowls, chilled in the freezer.

---

1 quart (1 l) pumpkin puree or canned pumpkin

2/3 cup (120 g) unrefined cane sugar, preferably organic, vanilla scented (see Notes on page 238)

1 teaspoon ground cinnamon, preferably Vietnamese cassia

1 teaspoon ground cloves

1/2 teaspoon ground allspice

1/2 teaspoon ground ginger

1/2 teaspoon pure vanilla extract

---

1. Combine all the ingredients in the blender or food processor and puree until smooth. Chill thoroughly.

2. At serving time, transfer the mixture to the ice cream maker and freeze according to the manufacturer's instructions. For best results, serve the sorbet in well-chilled bowls as soon as it is frozen. Do not re-freeze.

TIP: Both cubed and pureed pumpkin freeze beautifully. When I have more pumpkins than I can use at the moment, I cut them up and steam them, puree the cooked mixture, and store it in an airtight container in the freezer for up to 3 months.

KAFFIR LIME SORBET

~ 8 servings ~

Although my "thriving" kaffir lime tree has never blossomed or bore fruit, it supplies me with an endless crop of shiny fresh leaves for making this simple, refreshing sorbet.

EQUIPMENT: An electric spice mill; an ice cream maker; 8 ice cream bowls, chilled in the freezer.

20 fresh kaffir lime leaves, minced (or use dried or frozen kaffir lime leaves, minced, or 2 tablespoons grated lime zest, preferable organic)

1/2 cup (100 g) unrefined cane sugar, preferably organic, vanilla scented (see Notes on page 238)

2 cups (500 ml) 1% milk

1 cup (250 ml) light cream or half-and-half

1. Combine the leaves or zest and 2 tablespoons of the sugar in the spice mill, and grind to a fine powder.

2. In a large saucepan, combine the milk, cream, ground lime-sugar mixture, and the remaining sugar. Stir to dissolve the sugar. Heat over medium heat, stirring from time to time, just until tiny bubbles form around the edges of the pan, 3 to 4 minutes. Remove from the heat and let steep, covered, for 1 hour. Then chill thoroughly.

3. At serving time, transfer the mixture to the ice cream maker and freeze according to the manufacturer's instructions. For best results, serve the sorbet in well-chilled bowls as soon as it is frozen. Do not re-freeze.

POMEGRANATE AND BUTTERMILK SORBET

∽ 8 servings ∽

This delicate, fruity sorbet—pastel-pretty and dotted with brilliant red pomegranate seeds—reminds me of a festive glass of pink Champagne. Come September, when our pomegranates ripen in Provence, this appears at the dinner table frequently. The touch of honey here is essential, bringing a depth of flavor that sugar alone cannot provide.

EQUIPMENT: A blender or a food processor; an ice cream maker; 8 ice cream bowls, chilled in the freezer.

1 fresh pomegranate

1 cup (250 ml) pomegranate juice (see Note)

2 cups (500 ml) buttermilk, shaken to blend

1/2 cup (125 ml) lavender honey or other mild, fragrant honey

1. Cut off the crown of the pomegranate. Quarter the fruit lengthwise, being careful not to cut the seeds. Place the sections in a bowl of water. Roll the sections around in the water to dislodge the seeds. Strain out the water and discard all but the seeds.

2. In the blender or food processor, combine the pomegranate juice, buttermilk, and honey and puree until smooth. Chill thoroughly.

3. Transfer the mixture to the ice cream maker and freeze according to the manufacturer's directions. For best results, serve the sorbet in well-chilled bowls as soon as it is frozen. Do not re-freeze. Garnish with the pomegranate seeds before serving.

NOTE: When shopping for pomegranate juice, select one that is a clear, bright red, not cloudy, or your sorbet may end up a drab, pale pinkish orange. We find the bright and colorful clarity and flavor of Pom brand the best.

I love watching pomegranates—known as grenade *in French—grow into big, fat, glistening fruit, literally bursting at the seams as they ripen. My favorite use is in a fresh fruit sorbet.*

APRICOT AND LAVENDER HONEY SORBET

~ 8 servings ~

In our orchard, we have a pair of on-again, off-again apricot trees that are super-productive one year, yielding nothing the next. But when they're on, they're on, and that's when the kitchen is filled with the fresh, tart aroma of this silky-soft fruit. I learned the trick of cracking the pits to reveal the delicious, almond-like kernels from Maryse Jourdan, a Provençal housewife with a remarkable repertoire of local specialties. The kernels infuse the sorbet with a touch of bitter almond flavor, while the hint of lavender honey on the tongue is surprising and luscious.

EQUIPMENT: A wire-mesh ball; a blender or a food processor; an ice cream maker; 8 ice cream bowls, chilled in the freezer.

1 pound (500 g) ripe apricots, pitted and halved (pits reserved)

1/2 cup (125 ml) lavender honey or other mild, fragrant honey

1 cup (250 ml) Greek-style plain whole-milk yogurt

1. Crack the apricot pits to reveal the almond-like kernel within. Place the kernels in the wire-mesh ball.

2. In a saucepan, combine the apricots, honey, 1/2 cup (125 ml) of water, and the kernels in the wire-mesh ball. Bring to a simmer over medium heat, stirring to dissolve the honey. Simmer gently for 10 minutes. Remove the wire-mesh ball and discard the kernels. Let the apricot mixture cool to room temperature.

3. In the blender or food processor, combine the apricot mixture and the yogurt and puree until smooth. Chill thoroughly.

4. At serving time, transfer the mixture to the ice cream maker and freeze according to the manufacturer's instructions. For best results, serve the sorbet in well-chilled bowls as soon as it is frozen. Do not re-freeze.

VARIATION: Replace the yogurt with 1 cup (250 ml) of apricot nectar.

ROASTED FIG SORBET

~ 8 servings ~

When figs are in season, they demand to be picked and consumed right away! (Though they do freeze beautifully—see the Tip on page 250.) This sorbet is on the menu from early to late autumn, when our figs ripen.

EQUIPMENT: A blender or a food processor; an ice-cream maker; 8 ice cream bowls, chilled in the freezer.

2 pounds (1 kg) fresh figs, stems trimmed and discarded, halved lengthwise

6 tablespoons unrefined cane sugar, preferably organic, vanilla scented (see Note on page 238)

Grated zest of 1 lemon, preferably organic

1 teaspoon fresh thyme leaves

2 tablespoon sweet red wine, such as port or a *vin doux naturel* from Rasteau

1 cup (250 ml) Greek-style plain whole-milk yogurt

2 tablespoons Invert Sugar Syrup (page 75) or light corn syrup

1. Center a rack in the oven. Preheat the oven to 400°F (200°C).

2. In a baking dish, combine the figs, sugar, lemon zest, thyme, and wine. Toss to blend. Place in the oven and roast, uncovered, until hot and bubbly, about 30 minutes. Transfer the mixture to a container and chill thoroughly.

3. At serving time, combine the roasted figs and their liquid, the yogurt, and the syrup in the blender or food processor, and puree. Transfer the mixture to the ice cream maker and freeze according to the manufacturer's instructions. For best results, serve the sorbet in well-chilled bowls as soon as it is frozen. Do not re-freeze.

BITTERSWEET CHOCOLATE AND HONEY
SORBET WITH CHOCOLATE NIBS

~ 8 servings ~

Bittersweet chocolate and honey are worthy partners, both forward and forceful flavors. The final flourish of chocolate nibs makes this a triple-threat dessert and a serious contender for Best Taste of the Week.

EQUIPMENT: An ice cream maker; 8 ice cream bowls, chilled in the freezer.

2/3 cup (160 ml) lavender honey or other mild, fragrant honey

1/2 teaspoon fine sea salt

1 cup (80 g) unsweetened Dutch-process cocoa powder

7 ounces (210 g) bittersweet chocolate, such as Valrhona Guanaja 70%, broken into pieces

1 teaspoon pure vanilla extract

2 tablespoons Invert Sugar Syrup (page 75) or light corn syrup

2 tablespoons chocolate nibs (see Note on page 252)

1. In a large saucepan, combine 2 cups (500 ml) of water with the honey, salt, and cocoa powder. Bring to a boil over high heat. Then reduce the heat to moderate and simmer for 1 minute, whisking constantly. The mixture should turn a shiny, deep brown.

2. Off the heat, add the chocolate pieces, vanilla extract, and syrup, and stir until the chocolate is thoroughly melted. Chill thoroughly.

3. Transfer the mixture to the ice cream maker and freeze according to the manufacturer's instructions. For best results, serve the sorbet as soon as it is frozen. Do not re-freeze. At serving time, transfer a scoop to each chilled bowl and garnish with the chocolate nibs.

THE SECRET: Since this sorbet will thaw quickly, serving it in chilled bowls will keep it firmer longer.

THE PANTRY

KUMQUAT CONSERVE

~ Makes 1 quart (1 l) ~

My faithful kumquat tree produces year-round, supplying me with the makings of this tangy jam-like conserve, which I love to serve with a platter of fresh goat's milk cheeses. Serve this at a dinner party and then send guests home with a special gift of a small jar of this treasure.

EQUIPMENT: Eight 1/2-cup (125 ml) canning jars with lids.

1 1/2 pounds (750 g) unblemished fresh kumquats

2 cups (500 ml) fresh blood orange, mandarin orange, or regular orange juice

1 cup (200 g) unrefined cane sugar, preferably organic, vanilla scented (see Note on page 283)

1. Stem the kumquats, halve them lengthwise, and remove and discard the seeds.

2. In a large saucepan, combine the kumquats, orange juice, and sugar. Bring to a simmer and cook, skimming the surface as needed, until the juice is thick and the kumquats are soft and translucent, about 1 hour. Skim off and discard any recalcitrant seeds that float to the surface. Let cool.

3. Transfer to the canning jars and secure the lids. (Store in the refrigerator for up to 2 weeks.)

The prize among my collection of citrus trees growing in giant clay pots is the kumquat tree, which needs to be kept indoors in a sunny spot during the winter months, yet manages to offer a steady supply of the tart, thick-skinned fruits the size of a giant olive.

GREEN SAUCE WITH HERBS, ANCHOVIES, AND CAPERS

~ Makes about 1 cup (250 ml) ~

My good friend Jeffrey Bergman kindly shared this gorgeous, pungent sauce during a visit to Provence. Drizzle this on grilled vegetables, fish, or meat. It's a regular guest at our summer table. And so is he!

1 large shallot, peeled, halved, and finely minced

1 tablespoon freshly squeezed lemon juice

1/2 teaspoon sea salt

1/4 teaspoon coarse, freshly ground black pepper

1 tablespoon cider vinegar, champagne vinegar, or white wine vinegar

6 anchovy fillets in oil, drained and minced (see Note)

2 tablespoons capers in vinegar, drained

1 1/4 cups (310 ml) lightly packed minced flat-leaf parsley leaves

2 tablespoons minced fresh chives

2 tablespoons packed minced fresh mint leaves

1 tablespoon packed minced fresh tarragon leaves

1/2 cup (125 ml) extra-virgin olive oil

1. In a bowl, combine the shallot, lemon juice, salt, pepper, and vinegar. Let sit for 10 minutes for the lemon juice and vinegar to soften the sharpness of the shallot.

2. Add the anchovies and capers, and stir to blend. Add all the minced herbs and stir to blend. Add the oil and stir to blend. Let sit for 1 to 2 hours to allow the flavors to meld. (Store in an airtight container in the refrigerator for up to 1 week.)

NOTE: A favorite brand of anchovies is Rustichella d'Abruzzo, imported from Italy. They can be found at specialty stores and in Patricia's Pantry at my Amazon Store, accessed via the home page of www.PatriciaWells.com.

HOMEMADE CURRY POWDER

~ Makes 1/3 cup (5 tablespoons) ~

The best way to ensure freshness with spice mixtures is to create your own concoctions. This is a favorite curry powder mix, one I keep on hand and use liberally during all seasons.

EQUIPMENT: An electric spice mill.

2 whole small dried red chiles

2 tablespoons whole coriander seeds

1 tablespoon whole cumin seeds

1 teaspoon black mustard seeds

1 teaspoon whole black peppercorns

1 teaspoon ground ginger

1 teaspoon ground turmeric

Freshly ground spices are fragrant and bold. Store-bought ground spices can be stale and dull.

1. In a small, dry skillet, combine the chiles, coriander seeds, cumin seeds, mustard seeds, and peppercorns and toast over medium heat, shaking the pan often to prevent burning, 2 to 3 minutes.

2. Combine the toasted spices, ginger, and turmeric in the spice mill, and grind to a fine powder. (Store in an airtight container in a cool place for up to 1 month.)

THE SECRET: Save the date! Every time I create my own spice mixture or open a jar of store-bought spices, I mark the date on the jar. This way I know that when 6 months or so have passed, it may be time to discard and start anew. I use the sniff test: if the spices still have a vibrant, fresh aroma, they are probably still fine to use. As always, freshness is imperative to good taste in cooking.

HOMEMADE CHICKEN STOCK

~ Makes 3 quarts (3 l) ~

With a good homemade chicken stock in the refrigerator or freezer, a cook can go anywhere. It's the building block of a great cuisine.

EQUIPMENT: A long-handled, two-pronged fork; a 10-quart (10 l) pasta pot fitted with a colander; a fine-mesh skimmer; dampened cheesecloth.

2 large onions, halved crosswise (do not peel)

4 whole cloves

1 large farm-fresh chicken (about 5 pounds; 2.5 kg), preferably organic and free-range

2 teaspoons coarse sea salt

4 carrots, scrubbed and cut crosswise into 1-inch (2.5 cm) pieces (do not peel)

1 plump, moist garlic head, halved crosswise (do not peel)

4 celery ribs

1 leek, white and tender green parts only, halved lengthwise, rinsed, and cut into 1-inch (2.5 cm) pieces

One 1-inch (2.5 cm) piece of fresh ginger, peeled

12 whole white peppercorns

1 bouquet garni: several fresh or dried bay leaves, fresh celery leaves, thyme sprigs, and parsley sprigs encased in a wire-mesh tea infuser or bound in a piece of cheesecloth

1. One at a time, spear the onion halves with the long-handled fork and hold them directly over a gas flame (or directly on an electric burner) until scorched. (Scorching the onions will give the

broth a richer flavor. The onion skins also give the stock a rich, golden color.) Stick a clove into each of the onion halves.

2. Place the chicken in the pasta pot and fill it with 5 quarts (5 l) of water. Add the onions, salt, carrots, garlic, celery, leek, ginger, peppercorns, and bouquet garni. Bring to a gentle simmer, uncovered, over moderate heat. Skim to remove any scum that rises to the surface. Add additional cold water to replace the water removed and continue skimming until the broth is clear. Simmer until the chicken is cooked, about 1 hour.

3. Remove the chicken from the pot. Remove the chicken meat from the carcass and reserve it for another use. Return the skin and the carcass to the pot. Continue cooking at a gentle simmer for another 2 1/2 hours.

4. Line a large colander with a double layer of dampened cheesecloth and place the colander over a large bowl. Ladle—do not pour—the liquid into the sieve to strain off any impurities. Discard the solids. Measure. If the stock exceeds 3 quarts (3 l), return it to moderate heat and reduce it. Transfer the stock to airtight containers. Let it cool slightly, then cover.

5. Refrigerate the stock. Once it has chilled, spoon off all traces of fat that have risen to the surface. (Store the stock in the refrigerator for up to 3 days, or in the freezer for up to 3 months.)

NOTES:

•For a clear stock, begin with cold water and bring it slowly to a simmer. Never allow a stock to boil or it will be cloudy, since the fat will emulsify. Cold water also aids in extracting greater flavor.

•For the first 30 minutes of cooking, skim off the impurities that rise to the surface as the stock simmers.

•Use a tall pot to limit evaporation. I always use a large pasta pot fitted with a colander, which makes it easy to remove the solid ingredients and begin to filter the stock.

VARIATION: Use 2 whole chicken carcasses rather than a whole raw chicken. The resulting stock will not have the same clean, fresh flavor, but it is worthy nonetheless. One can also use about 4 pounds (2 kg) of inexpensive chicken necks and backs to prepare the stock.

HOMEMADE VEGETABLE STOCK

~ Makes 3 quarts (3 l) ~

I love it when my kitchen is "active," meaning I am cooking every day, morning, noon, and night. That's when I gather all the vegetable trimmings to prepare a rich stock. This recipe is just a template. The possibilities are endless: Use whatever well-scrubbed peels, ends, and scraps you may have from most vegetables. I prefer using celery and root vegetables such as carrots and onions, and avoid using such cruciferous vegetables as cabbage and broccoli, which can overpower the stock. Here one is looking for a gentle, background flavor.

EQUIPMENT: A long, handled, 2-pronged fork; a 10-quart (10 l) pasta pot fitted with a colander; dampened cheesecloth.

2 large onions, halved lengthwise (do not peel)

4 whole cloves

1 teaspoon coarse sea salt

4 carrots, scrubbed and cut crosswise into 1-inch (2.5 cm) pieces (do not peel)

1 plump, moist garlic head, halved crosswise (do not peel)

4 celery ribs, with leaves

1 leek, white and tender green parts only, halved lengthwise, rinsed, and cut into 1-inch (2.5 cm) pieces

One 1-inch (2.5 cm) piece of fresh ginger, peeled

6 black peppercorns

1 bouquet garni: several fresh or dried bay leaves, celery leaves, thyme sprigs, and parsley sprigs encased in a wire-mesh tea infuser or bound in a piece of cheesecloth

1. One at a time, spear the onion halves with the long-handled fork and hold them directly over a gas flame (or directly on an electric burner) until scorched. (Scorching the onions will give the broth a richer flavor. The onion skins also give the stock a rich, golden color.) Stick a clove into each of the onion halves.

2. Place the onions in the pasta pot, and add the salt, carrots, garlic, celery, leek, ginger, peppercorns, and bouquet garni. Fill the pot with 5 quarts (5 l) of water. Bring to a boil. Lower the heat and simmer, uncovered, for about 45 minutes. At this point, lift the colander out of the pot and discard the solids.

3. Line a large colander with a double layer of dampened cheesecloth and place the colander over a large bowl. Ladle—do not pour—the liquid into the sieve to strain off any impurities. Discard the solids. Measure. If the stock exceeds 3 quarts (3 l), return it to moderate heat and reduce it.

4. Transfer the stock to airtight containers and let it cool slightly. Then cover and refrigerate the stock. (Store the stock in the refrigerator for up to 3 days, or in the freezer for up to 3 months.)

SAVORY TOMATO MARMALADE

~ Makes 1 1/2 cups (375 ml) ~

Our friend Yale the analyst was visiting one summer and asked if we couldn't make a tomato marmalade, one to spoon over toast, pair with a thick slice of fresh tomato, or use as a relish for roasted vegetables, meats, poultry, or fish. We set out immediately and came up with this mildly tangy, slightly sweet, savory marmalade. For our first effort, we used giant yellow Ananas tomatoes, but now we prepare the same relish with both giant red beefsteak tomatoes and Green Zebra tomatoes, for a trio of colorful condiments.

EQUIPMENT: A large sieve.

1 small onion, peeled and cubed

2 plump, moist garlic cloves, peeled, halved, green germ removed, and minced

2 tablespoons extra-virgin olive oil

1/2 teaspoon fine sea salt

2 pounds (1 kg) garden-fresh tomatoes, cored, peeled, and cubed

1 tablespoon tomato vinegar, sherry vinegar, or balsamic vinegar

2 tablespoons sugar

Ground chile pepper to taste (optional)

1. In a saucepan, combine the onion, garlic, oil, and salt and sweat—cook, covered over low heat—until the onions are soft and translucent, about 10 minutes. Add the tomatoes, vinegar, and sugar. Simmer, uncovered, for 15 minutes. Strain through the sieve set over a bowl, reserving the juices.

2. Return the juices to the saucepan and reduce over high heat until thick and syrupy, 3 to 4 minutes. Pour the syrup over the tomatoes in the sieve. Let drain for a few minutes. Season with chile pepper to taste. Transfer the marmalade to an airtight container. Any liquid that drained from the tomatoes can be used in soups or sauces. (Store in an airtight container in the refrigerator for up to 3 days.)

BASIL-ARUGULA SAUCE

~ Makes 1 1/2 cups (375 ml) ~

When markets and gardens overflow with these two summertime treasures, go for it! I love to serve this with Fresh White Beans with Garlic and Basil Arugula-Sauce (page 143) or as a sauce for pasta, to or add a dollop to my *soupe au pistou* both summer and winter (page 85).

EQUIPMENT: A mortar and pestle, or a food processor fitted with a small bowl or a blender.

2 plump, moist garlic cloves, peeled, halved, green germ removed, and minced

1/4 teaspoon fine sea salt

4 cups (20 g) loosely packed fresh basil leaves

8 cups (80 g) loosely packed fresh arugula leaves

1/4 cup (60 ml) extra-virgin olive oil

1. *By hand:* Place the garlic and salt in a mortar and mash with a pestle to form a paste. Be patient and work slowly and evenly. Add the basil and arugula, little by little, pounding and turning the pestle with a grinding motion to form a paste. Slowly add the oil, turning the pestle with a grinding motion until all the oil has been used. The sauce will not form an emulsion, like a mayonnaise, but rather bits of the leaves will remain suspended in the oil. Taste for seasoning. *In a food processor or a blender:* Place the garlic, salt, basil, and arugula in the bowl of a food processor or blender, and process to a paste. With the machine running, slowly add the oil through the feed tube. The sauce will be thick and smooth. Taste for seasoning.

2. Transfer the sauce to a small bowl. Stir again before serving. (The sauce can be stored, covered and refrigerated, for 3 days, or frozen for up to 6 months. Bring to room temperature and stir again before serving.)

CLARIFIED BUTTER

~ Makes about 6 tablespoons (90 g) ~

What is clarified butter? And why bother? Clarified butter is butter that has the milk solids and water removed. This gives it a much higher smoking point than regular butter and allows you to cook at a higher temperature without burning. Without the milk solids, clarified butter can also be kept fresher longer than non-clarified butter. I use it, often in conjunction with a touch of oil, when cooking foods that I want to cook at a high heat without burning, such as the Ham and Cheese Squares with Cornichons (page 11).

EQUIPMENT: A double boiler or a microwave oven; a fine-mesh sieve; dampened cheesecloth.

8 tablespoons (125 g) unsalted butter

1. Cut the butter into small pieces and place them in the top of a double boiler set over simmering water. When the butter has melted, increase the heat to moderate and allow the butter to simmer until it stops crackling, an indication that the butter is beginning to "fry." Remove the pan from the heat and allow the residue to settle to the bottom of the pan; there should be a layer of milk solids on the bottom and a layer of foam on top.

2. Alternatively, prepare in the microwave: Place the butter in a 1 1/2-quart (1.5 l) microwave-safe dish (do not use a smaller container or the butter will splatter all over the oven). Cover loosely with paper towels. Microwave at full power for 2 1/2 minutes. Remove from the oven and allow the residue to settle to the bottom of the dish; there should be a layer of milk solids on the bottom and a layer of foam on top.

3. With a spoon, skim off and discard the top layer of foam. Line a fine-mesh sieve with dampened cheesecloth and slowly strain the melted butter into a container, discarding the milky solids that remain. (Store in an airtight container in the refrigerator for up to 1 month.)

FIRE SALT

~ Makes about 6 tablespoons ~

I love spice and I love salt, so why not put the two together in a salt grinder? I keep this at hand for whenever I want to add a touch of each to my food, such as on pizza or pasta. You can make this as mild or as spicy as you like by adjusting the proportions.

EQUIPMENT: An electric spice mill; a salt grinder.

2 ounces (60 g) dried long red chiles, trimmed and coarsely chopped

3 tablespoons coarse sea salt

In the spice mill, coarsely chop the chiles. In a small bowl, combine the ground chiles and the salt. Transfer to the salt grinder. (Use within 6 months. After that, the flavors will begin to fade.)

VIETNAMESE DIPPING SAUCE

~ Makes 3/4 cup (185 ml) ~

I am never without this sauce in my refrigerator, for dipping with raw or marinated fish or for my favorite local Vietnamese carry-out spring rolls.

EQUIPMENT: A mini food processor or a standard food processor fitted with a small bowl; a small jar with a lid.

2 plump, moist garlic cloves, peeled, halved, green germ removed

1 fresh or dried red bird's eye chile

3 tablespoons Vietnamese fish sauce, preferably Red Boat brand (see Note on 56)

3 tablespoons freshly squeezed lime or lemon juice

2 tablespoons sugar

In the food processor, mince the garlic and chile. Add the fish sauce, citrus juice, sugar, and 1/2 cup (125 ml) of water. Pulse to blend. Taste for seasoning. Transfer to the jar and tighten the lid. (Store in the refrigerator for up to 1 week.)

BLITZ PUFF PASTRY

~ Makes about 1 2/3 pounds (800 g) pastry, enough for 2 tarts ~

As much as I love to teach cooking, I also love to attend cooking classes to improve my own culinary techniques. Several years ago, my husband, Walter, and I enrolled in several weeklong bread-baking sessions at the San Francisco Baking Institute. During the wood-oven class we were reunited with this amazingly simple "blitz" puff pastry, a version of which we made together years ago and then sort of forgot. While classic puff pastry can take hours of labor, this quick one can be made, start to finish, in just two hours. And that's not two hours of constant work—just a few minutes here and there. The dough is incredibly pliable and easy to roll out, and it's a treat to have a batch in the refrigerator for making pastries and appetizers; it can easily be frozen, too. The malt powder or flakes helps with browning and adds a deeper, distinctive flavor to the pastry, while the lemon juice adds a nice touch of acidity to the dough, prevents it from darkening before baking, and also makes the dough more tender.

EQUIPMENT: A heavy-duty mixer fitted with a paddle.

2 1/2 cups (360 g) unbleached, all-purpose flour

16 tablespoons (250 g) unsalted butter, chilled and cubed

2 teaspoons fine sea salt

2 teaspoons malt powder or malt flakes (see Note)

3/4 cup (185 ml) ice water

2 teaspoons lemon juice

1. In the bowl of the mixer, combine the flour, butter, salt, and malt powder. Mix at low speed until the butter is evenly distributed but large chunks are still visible, about 30 seconds.

2. Combine the ice water and lemon juice. Add the lemon water to the flour mixture all at once, mixing at low speed just until the dough forms a ball, about 10 seconds. Do not over mix. The dough will be wet and shaggy.

3. Transfer the dough to a generously floured, clean work surface. Gather the dough into a ball. Flatten it into a 6-inch (15 cm) square. Wrap the dough in foil. Refrigerate it for at least 20 minutes.

4. Lightly flour a clean work surface. Remove the dough from the refrigerator and roll it into a 6 x 18-inch (15 x 45 cm) rectangle. Fold the dough in thirds, resulting in a square. Repeat 1 more time, rolling the dough into a rectangle, folding it in thirds. Wrap the dough in foil and refrigerate it for at least 20 minutes.

5. Remove the dough from the refrigerator and roll and fold the dough a third time. Wrap the dough in foil and refrigerate for at least 20 minutes.

6. Remove the dough from the refrigerator and roll and fold the dough a fourth time. Wrap the dough in the foil and refrigerate for at least 20 minutes.

7. Remove the dough from the refrigerator and roll and fold the dough a fifth and final time. Cover and refrigerate for 1 hour. The dough is ready to use. If the dough is not to be used right away, I generally roll it out to desired sizes for tarts or various-size small pastry rounds and refrigerate or freeze for future use. Wrapped securely, the dough can be stored in the refrigerator for 1 week or the freezer for 1 month.

NOTE: Malt powder, also known as diastatic malt powder, can be found in Patricia's Pantry at my Amazon Store, accessed via the home page of www.PatriciaWells.com.

ROVENCE

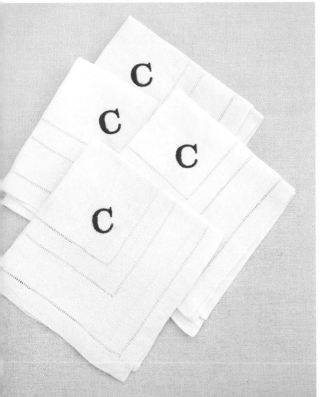

For me, a festive table is not completely outfitted unless knife rests are part of the table setting. My collection is made up of various materials, colors, sizes, and themes. Fish for a fish course, autumn leaves for a fall feast, herbs for a vegetarian meal, and the ubiquitous cigale, or cricket, for a summer party in Provence.

I have been collecting napkin rings, mostly in silver or silverplate, at flea markets for decades. As with linens monogrammed with someone else's initials, I like to think about what kind of time Octave, or Yvonne, or "J" had at the table. I often assign dinner guests a personality, and when they return, they ask to become that mystery guest once again.

Flea markets are great places to find antique tools that have mostly been replaced by modern-day equivalents. It's fun to guess what each tool might be used for: one for unearthing potatoes, another for cutting fragrant lavender, and yet another special tool for coaxing fresh winter black truffles from the ground.

I often harvest more fresh herbs than I may use for a dish and arrange the excess as a small bouquet for the kitchen counter.

Just as I love listening to music written, played, or sung by someone I know, I cherish using household objects—in both the kitchen and at the table—hand-crafted by someone I know. I long collected the sturdy, colorful faïence from the Atelier Bernard in Apt in Provence (now, alas, no longer in business), as well as other local potters.

Whenever I find a fine collection of simple antique napkins—as here, lovely linen cocktail napkins—I take them to my local seamstress for a monogram. Here it's a simple "C" for the name of our farm, Chanteduc.

MY PREFERRED WINE IMPORTERS

Here's a list of my preferred individuals importing wines from France to the United States. I always encourage my students to "buy by the back label," that is, to look at the back label on any wine bottle to see who the importer is. For novice wine tasters in particular, I advise students to take this list into a wine store and ask the merchant, "Do you have any wines from any of these importers?" These importers can be trusted, and once you begin connecting importers' names to wines you love, you're on your way. Many of them have extraordinarily excellent and informative websites, worth a tour on their own.

ERIC SOLOMON

(704) 358-1565

www.europeancellars.com

info@europeancellars.com

Specializing in wines from Spain and France, including Clos Chanteduc Côtes-du-Rhône; and Domaine de la Janasse and Domaine de Marcoux in Châteauneuf-du-Pape.

KERMIT LYNCH WINE MERCHANT

(510) 524-1524

www.kermitlynch.com

info@kermitlynch.com

Specializing in wines from Italy and France, including Auguste Clape in Cornas; Domaine Coche-Dury and Antoine Jobard in Burgundy; and Mas Champart in the Languedoc.

NORTH BERKELEY WINE

(510) 848-8910 or (800) 266-6585

www.northberkeleyimports.com

retail@northberkeleywine.com

Specializing in wines from Chile, Italy, and France, including Le Cos du Caillou and Clos du Mont Olivet in Châteauneuf-du-Pape; Martinelle in Beaumes de Venise; and Domaine la Bouïssière in Gigondas.

CHRISTOPHER CANNAN

(818) 908-9509

www.Europvin.com

europvin@europvin.com

Specializing in wines from Spain, Portugal, Italy, Hungary, and France, including Château des Tour in Vacqueyras; Vieille Julienne and Château Rayas in Châteauneuf-du-Pape; and Domaine Anne Gros in Vosne-Romanée.

LOUIS/DRESSNER SELECTIONS

(212) 334-8191

www.louisdressner.com

info@louisdressner.com

Specializing in wines from throughout Europe, including Oratoire Saint Martin and Domaine Marcel Richaud in Cairanne; Château d'Oupia in Minervois; and Jean Thévenet/Domaine de la Bongran in Burgundy.

ROBERT KACHER

(212) 239-1275

www.robertkacherselections.com

rks@robertkacherselections.com

Specializing in wines from Portugal, Argentina, and France, including Domaine Santa Duc in Gigondas; Domaine Michel and Stéphane Ogier and Domaine Jamet in Côte-Rôtie.

KYSELA PÈRE ET FILS

(540) 722-9258

www.kysela.com

fran.k@kysela.com

Specializing in wines from Australia, New Zealand, the United States, Argentina, and Europe, including Domaine Grand Veneur and Domaine de la Mordorée in the southern Rhône.

MARTINE'S WINES

(415) 883-0400 or (800) 344-1801

www.martineswines.com

info@mwines.com

Specializing in wines from France, including Château Rayas in Châteauneuf-du-Pape, Château de Fonsalette in the Côtes-du-Rhône; Château des Tours in Vacqueyras; and Domaine Georges Vernay in the northern Rhône.

MICHAEL SKURNIK

(516) 677-9300

www.skurnikwines.com

info@skurnikwines.com

Specializing in wines from France, particularly those selected by Daniel Johnnes, who is also wine director for Daniel Boulud in New York City, with wines including Saint Préfert in Châteauneuf-du-Pape; Grange des Pères in the Languedoc; and Les Héritiers du Comte Lafon in Burgundy.

VINEYARD BRANDS

(205) 980-8802

www.vineyardbrands.com

vb@vineyardbrands.com

Specializing in wines from Chile, New Zealand, South Africa, Spain, Italy, and France, including a collection of wines from Château de Beaucastel in Châteauneuf-du-Pape and the southern Rhône; Dauvissat in Chablis; and Salon in Champagne.

PETER WEYGANDT

(610) 486-0700

www.weygandtmetzler.com

peter@weygandtmetzler.com

Specializing in wines from Austria, Australia, Germany, Italy, and France, including Domaine Gérard Charvin and Raymond Usseglio in Châteauneuf-du-Pape; and Daniel and Denis Alary in Cairanne.

When I wrote The Food Lover's Guide to Paris, *first published in 1984, the French translated it as* Le Paris Gourmand. *A lovely couple who owned a sign shop in Paris then made me my own "street" sign, something I have treasured ever since!*

ACKNOWLEDGMENTS

When years of pleasure, years of labor go into a work such as this, the memory of all the gracious friends who touched my life along the way simply makes me smile. The menu planning together, the shopping, the joy of cooking, and the final satisfaction of sitting down at table to celebrate and enjoy our efforts are all integral parts of our lives.

Every student who has passed through my kitchens since cooking classes first began in 1995 is silently acknowledged here. With many I have formed long and lasting friendships, among them Andrew Axilrod, John Braver, Marcella Butler, Anne and Allen Dick, Betsy Fox, Casey Gaines, Nancy Hachisu, Brian Huggler, Lee Isgur, Sandy Jaffee, Diane Madden, Todd Murray, Judy Nocerino, Kyle Kuvalanka, Jeffrey Sobell, and Virginia Ward.

In Paris, so many friends and merchants have improved my life immensely, including the staff at the renowned bakery Poilâne, as well as everyone at La Dernière Goutte wine shop, especially Juan Sanchez and Patty Lurie. Marie Quatrehomme and her bounteous cheese shop supplies treasures for our kitchen and table, while the local vegetables and fruits from Joël Thiébault just make every dish taste better. And thank you, Jean-Bernard Guilhien, my Rue du Bac butcher, for supplying such incredible beef for our favored *daube*.

In both Paris and Provence, good friends Jeffrey and Katherine Bergman have joyfully tested and tasted with us through the seasons. For all the treasures from our Provençal garden I thank Cédric Ganichot, and the same for greengrocers Corrine and Josiane Meliani, who fill in the blanks throughout the year, butchers Gilles Diglé and the Raymonds, Jean-Claude and Stéphane, for all the incredible local lamb and rabbit, and Didier Célerin, for his amazing farm-raised chickens. Josiane and Christian Déal have been part of our food family for years, and our kitchen and table would be far less rich without the magnificent selections from their cheese shop, Lou Canesteou. We are blessed with dedicated fish merchants in Provence, including Eliane and Aymer Berenger and Pierline and Fabien Borecki. And there is no way I can offer enough thanks and gratitude to Yveline Lanciel and Annie Tourance, our trusted "kitchen angels."

On the office side of life, great friend and super assistant Emily Buchanan offers priceless aid, while back in New York I want to thank my agent Amanda Urban, editor Cassie Jones, and her assistant, Kara Zauberman. Thank you, designer Lorie Pagnozzi. Also at William Morrow, thanks to Liate Stehlik, Lynn Grady, Andy Dodds, and Tavia Kowalchuk. Thank you, as well, Jonathan Burnham, publisher of Harper.

And wherever I am, the best person in the kitchen is my loving partner, Walter Wells.

Patricia Wells

INDEX